Crime and Punishment

FYODOR DOSTOEVSKY

Level 6

Retold by Nancy Taylor
Series Editors: Andy Hopkins and Jocelyn Potter

Pearson Education Limited
Edinburgh Gate, Harlow,
Essex CM20 2JE, England
and Associated Companies throughout the world.

ISBN 978-1-4058-8262-0

First published 2006
This edition published 2008

Text copyright © Pearson Education Ltd 2008

7

Typeset by Graphicraft Limited, Hong Kong
Set in 11/14pt Bembo
Printed in China
SWTC/07

Produced for the Publishers by
Graphicraft Productions Limited, Dartford, UK

Published by Pearson Education Ltd

Every effort has been made to trace the copyright holders and we apologise in advance
for any unintentional omissions. We would be pleased to insert the appropriate
acknowledgement in any subsequent edition of this publication.

Contents

Introduction

'Is it a crime to kill a disgusting old moneylender who, like a louse, lived on the blood of her victims? I'm ready to confess that I killed her, but I won't call my act a crime.'

Rodion Romanovitch Raskolnikoff, the main character in *Crime and Punishment*, speaks these words towards the end of the book. He will admit that he is responsible for a murder, but he will not accept society's interpretation of his motives. Even after his confession, this complex character continues his long struggle to explain his crime – especially to himself.

Raskolnikoff, a young intellectual in nineteenth-century Russia, has been forced to abandon his university studies because of lack of money. He withdraws from real life and – poor and lonely in his small featureless room – he develops a theory to explain the difference between the goals and principles of ordinary and extraordinary men.

In a rather confused state – caused partly by his extreme poverty – he combines this theory with his need for money, his desire to do good and his superstitious beliefs, and puts together a plan to murder a greedy old moneylender and to become 'extraordinary'. He carries out his plan, but that is only the beginning of the story. After his great crime, Raskolnikoff must understand his motives and explain them to himself and to the people he respects, which he is never able to do to his (or our) complete satisfaction.

Raskolnikoff is not a typical hero. Although he is young, intelligent and handsome, he is difficult to like. He is a murderer and, in addition, he does not seem to like being around people. Instead, he chooses to ignore the feelings and needs of others while he isolates himself and struggles to understand his place in the world. But there is another side to Raskolnikoff, which makes him interesting. He is sympathetic and generous to people in need, and he recognizes the goodness and bravery in the lives of people who are unselfish and pure. Because of this split personality, it is not easy to predict how he will act in any particular situation, nor what will happen to him in the end.

Raskolnikoff lives in a nineteenth-century world, but his psychological battles are relevant to twenty-first century readers. Why does such an intelligent young man become a killer? How does he feel as he commits not one, but two violent murders? How does he live with his conscience after he carries out his bloody deed? Dostoyevsky invites you to accompany Raskolnikoff on his modern journey of self-discovery.

Fyodor Mikhailovich Dostoyevsky is regarded by many literary experts as the greatest Russian novelist that ever lived, and possibly the most important influence on all of twentieth-century western literature. In addition to shaping our present-day concept of the novel, his ideas also influenced modern psychology, religious theory and literary criticism.

His effect on the modern novel can be seen especially among American writers, many of whom deal with Dostoyevsky's idea of the 'underground hero', a man who feels cut off from the meaning of life in a world outside his control. Dostoyevsky's works are also significant because of his accurate prediction of how the leaders of Russia's revolution would behave when they came to power.

Born in Moscow in 1821, Dostoyevsky was the son of a retired military doctor who, though loving, was a very strict authority figure. His mother, on the other hand, was cultured, kind and generous to her children. Different from others of their class, Dostoyevsky's family had an old-fashioned, serious respect for religion, an attitude that remained with the writer throughout his life. But although the family was relatively rich and young Dostoyevsky had a comfortable life, he also had to face difficult crises. His mother died in 1837, and his father is believed to have been murdered by his own servants in 1839. Following his father's orders, Dostoyevsky was at this time at a military school studying to be an army engineer. He successfully completed this course of studies in 1843, but rejected a military career to pursue his dream of being a writer.

He was almost immediately recognized as a talented new writer when his short story *Poor Folk* was published in 1846. The story was praised for its accurate description of the psychological effects of poverty, but his other work in the 1840s was less warmly received. Nevertheless, these early stories show his interest in exploring the minds of people with split personalities and other psychological problems.

Dostoyevsky's life altered dramatically in 1847 when he joined the Petrashevsky Circle, a group of young intellectuals who were interested in changing Russian society to make it a better place for all classes of people. He eventually joined a related, secret group which supported more revolutionary ideas, and in 1849 Dostoyevsky and other members of the group were arrested because they were considered to be a threat to the government. After eight months in prison, these young men narrowly escaped a death sentence and were sent to Siberia for four years' hard labour, followed by almost five more years as soldiers. These experiences led Dostoyevsky to reconfirm his loyalty to the beliefs and values of the Russian Orthodox Church and to reject both Western political ideas and a more liberal, modern approach to religion as a model for Russian society. They also strengthened his belief in the basic goodness of ordinary people.

Dostoyevsky returned to St Petersburg in 1859 with his wife, whom he had met while he was a soldier, ready to begin the major phase of his career in literature. At first he worked with his brother, Mikhail, on two influential journals which questioned popular political theories, attacked modern business practices and supported ideas of individual freedom and responsibility.

After Mikhail's death, he wrote from personal experience about the horrors of prison camps, about cruel guards, about the evil minds of criminals, and about decent men who were sent to prison because of their political or religious opinions. His book *Notes from the Underground* (1864) shows a character at war with the wickedness of the modern scientific world and includes the basis for many of the ideas found in his greatest novels.

But before writing those important works, Dostoyevsky travelled between Russia and Western Europe for a number of years, studying the culture he admired and businesses that emphasized profit, which he hated. One of his reasons for going to Europe was to escape from huge debts that he had built up as a result of his love of playing cards. He was able to return to Russia permanently in 1871 after writing several hugely successful novels and marrying again in 1867, following the death of his first wife. His second wife worked as his secretary and also put his finances in order.

The novels published before 1871 include *The Gambler* (1866) and two of his greatest books: *Crime and Punishment* (1866) and *The Idiot* (1868). These were followed by another highly praised work, *The Devils* (1872), and *An Adolescent* (1875), before the book in which most experts think Dostoyevsky's art reached its peak: *The Brothers Karamazov* (1880). This powerful story of family relationships includes all the topics most important to the author: the battle between love and hate, and between faith and lack of faith; the question of whether or not God exists; the dangers of political systems and the attempt to engineer human happiness; the struggles between parents and children, and the difference between human capabilities and achievements.

Since his death in St Petersburg in 1881, Dostoyevsky's world-wide fame and literary reputation have continued to grow. No other nineteenth-century writer understands and explores the mysteries of the human soul so systematically and completely, and no other writer of that period captures the mood and tone of the decades that followed so successfully. In fact, some experts have described the second half of the twentieth century as 'Dostoyevskian'. Outside Russia, at least, he has remained the most widely-read and highly-regarded Russian novelist of his time.

Crime and Punishment is typically Dostoyevskian for several reasons. First of all, it explores the nature of good and evil through the behaviour and beliefs of Raskolnikoff, a very complex character who struggles to find redemption through suffering. Secondly, it shows the horrors of poverty and crime in a modern city and the shame of living in a society which ignores the poor. Lastly, it has a dramatic, powerful plot which is both challenging and entertaining for the reader. Because it deals with the human struggle to understand the meaning of life, it is not surprising that this novel continues to be read, and that it has been adapted repeatedly for both film and television.

List of Main Characters

RODION ROMANOVITCH RASKOLNIKOFF, student and murderer
PULCHERIA ALEXANDROVNA, mother of murderer
DOUNIA ROMANOVNA, sister of murderer
DMITRI PROKOVITCH RAZOUMIKHIN, friend of murderer
PETER PETROVITCH LOOSHIN, Dounia's future husband

ALENA IVANOVNA, moneylender
ELIZABETH, stepsister and servant of moneylender

PORPHYRIUS PETROVITCH, magistrate
ELIA PETROVITCH POWDER, police officer

MARMELADOFF, drunkard
CATHERINE IVANOVNA, drunkard's wife
SONIA SEMENOVNA, prostitute, drunkard's daughter
POLENKA, eldest daughter of Catherine Ivanovna

ARCADIUS IVANOVITCH SVIDRIGAÏLOFF, rich widower
MARFA PETROVNA, Svidrigaïloff's wife

NASTASIA, servant
ZOSIMOFF, young doctor
NIKOLA and DMITRI, painters

Chapter 1 The Crime

One hot evening early in July, a worried-looking young man walked out of the small room he rented in a large five-storey house in one of the poorest sections of St Petersburg. He hurried down the stairs and past his landlady's open door, feeling fortunate to reach the street without attracting her attention since he owed her money.

The young man, Rodion Romanovitch Raskolnikoff, had not been the victim of great misfortune or tragedy, although his appearance might lead the observer to that conclusion. Instead, his suffering was the result of a state of nervous depression which had caused him to abandon his university studies, his work, and society in general. He spent his days shut away in his tiny room, avoiding not only his landlady, but every human face.

'Why should I be worried about such insignificant concerns as paying the rent or facing my landlady's anger when I'm plotting something extraordinary?' thought Raskolnikoff with a strange smile. 'What do I have to fear from everyday life?' He turned in the direction of the Haymarket, a neighbourhood at the heart of St Petersburg occupied by the struggling lower classes.

Raskolnikoff felt disgusted by the sights and smells around him: men drunk outside cheap taverns, prostitutes waiting on street corners, young children running wild. He fitted into this crowd because, like most people here, he was poorly dressed and appeared to need a good meal. A closer look at the young man, though, revealed a handsome, intelligent face with fine dark eyes and thick dark brown hair. He was also above average in height, with a thin but strong body.

Suddenly he heard a loud voice shout, 'Look at the gentleman in the fine top hat! Who does he think he is?'

Raskolnikoff quickly removed his hat and examined it. It had been expensive and very smart when it was new, but now it was old, dirty and out of fashion. 'I suspected something like this,' Raskolnikoff thought, cursing himself. 'My ridiculous hat would be remembered even some time after the event, and it might provide a clue. No one must notice me.'

He was at his destination, exactly 730 steps from his apartment building. He had counted the steps weeks ago when his plan was still a shadowy dream, but now he surprised himself by practising what he planned to do on the fatal day.

His heart beat loudly and his limbs trembled as he stood facing an enormous building which had been divided into numerous small flats. There was a constant stream of residents – carpenters, cooks, office clerks and others – going in and out of the two main entrances. Raskolnikoff joined the crowd and, without attracting attention, entered the building and quickly climbed the dark, narrow stairs.

'Calm down!' he told himself. 'If I'm nervous now, what will I be like on the day I put my plan into action?'

As he reached the fourth floor, he had to allow two men carrying a large table to pass him. They were emptying one of the two flats on that level.

'The Germans must be moving out,' thought Raskolnikoff, as he approached the other flat. 'Until a new occupant is found, the old lady will be the only resident on this floor.' He rang her tin bell and noticed the faint sound it made inside her flat.

After a minute or two the door was opened slightly, revealing the small, sharp eyes of the old moneylender in the shadowy entrance. When she recognized the young man, Alena Ivanovna opened the door; Raskolnikoff had visited her before with objects to pawn.

Inside the humble apartment, Raskolnikoff could see the old woman more clearly. She was a thin little creature of sixty, with a sharp nose and eyes bright with suspicion. Her head was uncovered and her ugly grey hair shone with oil. In spite of the July heat, she was wearing an old rag wrapped around her neck and a cheap piece of fur across her shoulders.

The young man bowed, remembering that he must be polite to this old woman if he expected her to open her door willingly to him on his next visit. 'Do you remember me, Alena Ivanovna? It's Raskolnikoff, the student who visited you a month ago. You gave me two roubles* for a ring.'

'I remember all my clients who still owe me money,' replied Alena Ivanovna rudely. Then she remained silent, which made Raskolnikoff even more nervous as he looked around her sitting room, trying to memorize anything that might affect his plan. The furniture was old, but clean and well polished, there were some inexpensive pictures on the walls, and there was a lamp burning in one corner in front of a picture of a saint.

'Her sister must look after this place,' thought Raskolnikoff. 'People say the old woman treats her like a servant.'

'What do you want?' the moneylender asked. 'Have you come to repay me the money I lent you?'

'No, I've brought something else to pawn. What will you give me for this silver watch? It belonged to my father.'

'It's not worth much,' said the old woman, as she looked at the watch. 'You can have a rouble and a half for the watch, minus thirty-five kopecks* that you owe me in interest: one rouble fifteen kopecks.'

'What! Is that all you intend to give me?'

'That's all that's due to you.'

'I'll take it because I must, but it's not a fair price,' Raskolnikoff complained.

He watched the old woman as she took out her keys and went into the bedroom, the only other room in the flat. He listened

* roubles, kopecks: Russian money

3

carefully as she unlocked a drawer and then something else –
perhaps a safe or a metal box.

After Alena Ivanovna handed the money to Raskolnikoff, he
began talking again. 'I may bring you a very good piece of silver
very soon. It's a pretty cigarette case.'

'I'll talk to you when you bring it. Good day.'

'Goodbye,' Raskolnikoff responded. 'You're always alone when
I come here. Is your sister never at home in the daytime?'

'Why is my sister any of your business?' demanded the old
woman.

'You're right, she isn't. I must go. You will . . . well . . .
goodbye, Alena Ivanovna.'

As he hurried down the stairs, Raskolnikoff was in a confused,
emotional state of mind. 'How disgusting! That woman is a nasty
creature, like an animal living in her dark hole, counting her
gold. But can I ever . . .? No, it's ridiculous, horrible! I'm not
capable of this deed, but it's all I can think of.'

Full of self-hatred, he needed to escape from his thoughts and,
with this in mind, he pushed past several drunkards and found
a seat in a dark, dirty corner of an inferior tavern. There, after
eating a cheap biscuit and quickly drinking a glass of beer, he felt
his brain begin to clear.

'What a fool I've been!' Raskolnikoff said to himself. 'I had no
reason to be upset. I simply needed some food and drink, and
now my head is clear again, and my plan is unchanged.'

His face looked bright, almost cheerful, as he glanced round
the room. There were very few men in the place, but one caught
his eye. This man, who had obviously been drinking steadily for
days, was over fifty, of medium height, with thin grey hair and
yellowish skin, a sign of an alcoholic. Though his clothes were
dirty and worn and his cheeks were unshaven, the man somehow
looked intelligent and enthusiastic; Raskolnikoff guessed that he
might be some kind of government official. The man stared at

Raskolnikoff, seemingly anxious to begin a conversation, and after several minutes he spoke in a loud, formal voice.

'Sir, allow me to introduce myself. I am Marmeladoff, a servant of the city of St Petersburg. Please permit me to exchange a few words with you. There is no one else worth talking to in this miserable place, but you, I can see, are an educated man – perhaps a government official like myself?'

'No, sir, I'm a student,' Raskolnikoff answered roughly, feeling annoyed by this disturbance.

Unfortunately for him, Marmeladoff, who was clearly not easily offended, picked up his glass and moved to a seat at the same table.

'Sir,' he began with a certain authority in his voice, 'have you ever spent a night floating on the Neva River in a boat?'

'No, I never have,' answered Raskolnikoff. 'Why?'

'That is where I have been sleeping for the last week.' He looked as if he had neither changed his clothes nor washed recently. Everyone in the place was listening now; although they knew Marmeladoff's story, they were not tired of it yet.

'But you're a government official,' shouted the owner of the tavern. 'Why aren't you at work, serving the good people of St Petersburg?'

'You ask why? Because I'm an animal, a louse. I have a young, educated wife, but she has no pity for me. If she could love me, I could be a man again, but I'm a failure. I've sold everything we possessed – even my wife's warm coat – so that I can have a drink. This good woman coughs blood and struggles to breathe, but she works from morning until night in a cold room with her three young children, trying to keep everything clean, trying to find food for them. I married her when she was a young widow with three mouths to feed and nowhere to go to.

'Can you understand, sir, what it means to have nowhere to go? I treated her well for a year, before I lost my job and started drinking again. Sonia, my own daughter by my first marriage – only a teenager herself but with no education – was forced to become a prostitute to provide food for my starving family. What else could she do? Catherine Ivanovna pushed her into the street, but when she returned with money, Catherine kissed her feet and comforted her. I feel their pain, but the more I feel, the more I drink – and then I suffer even more.

'Now Sonia carries the yellow card – a licence from the police to sell her body. Our landlady will not permit her to live in our room, but she brings us any money she has been able to earn.

'Oh, sir, listen!' begged Marmeladoff. 'Perhaps, like these others, you think my life is a great comedy, but my troubles don't amuse me. They stab me in the heart. Five days ago I stole Catherine's last rouble, and yesterday I borrowed Sonia's last few kopecks to pay for drink. Now I have nothing left. Can you still be sympathetic after hearing of my cruel behaviour?

'But one day I will find peace. One day God will forgive Sonia because she sacrificed everything to help those little children. And he'll forgive me and all other drunkards because we know we don't deserve his love. He will open his arms and receive us into his kingdom.'

Marmeladoff fell against his chair, exhausted by his long speech. There was clapping from the other drunkards, but it soon changed back into laughter and abuse.

'Sir, take me away from these uneducated creatures. It's time to return to Catherine Ivanovna,' the older man said.

Raskolnikoff assisted Marmeladoff in his unsteady walk to his house, and up the dark stairs to the fourth floor, where they looked through an open door into a miserable, crowded room. The noise, smoke and terrible smells from the neighbours' rooms crept into every corner of this comfortless place.

Catherine Ivanovna had been a beautiful woman but now, although she was not even thirty years old, her health was gone and she looked ill and desperate. Her little children, aged four, five and ten, were poorly dressed, hungry for food and for kindness. They lived in fear of their mother, but she was everything to them, and they watched her with big, tearful eyes, never sure of her mood or her treatment of them.

The mother of these poor babies suddenly noticed her husband kneeling outside her door. 'You've come back!' she cried in a voice shaking with anger. 'You devil! Where's my money? Empty your pockets! Don't you have a single kopeck on you?'

She seized her husband by the hair and dragged him on his hands and knees into the room, shouting abuse at him with every kick and every smack she gave him. The children hid in the corner, frightened almost to death, although scenes like this were clearly familiar to them.

'Look at the children! They're starving! And you, sir, aren't you ashamed to come here? Has he bought drinks for you, too? Get out!' she screamed at Raskolnikoff.

The younger man did not wait to be told again, and left the room. But on his way out, without attracting anyone's notice, Raskolnikoff laid the few kopecks remaining in his pocket on a shelf beside the window.

As soon as he was alone he regretted his generous gesture. 'How stupid! Now I have almost no money and no one to help me. At least that family have Sonia. I imagine they cried when they sent her into the street with her yellow card, but now they're used to her situation. Man's a coward and can get used to anything.' He thought for a minute. 'But if man isn't a coward, he should fight against every fear and every injustice that stand in his way.'

♦

After a sleepless night, Raskolnikoff woke very late the next morning and lay in bed angrily examining his miserable room.

It was no more than two metres wide with an unusually low ceiling – really, not much bigger than a cupboard. He had a couple of old wooden chairs, a painted table and an ugly sofa covered in rags which served as his bed. His books and papers in one corner were covered in dust; he had not done any studying or teaching for months.

'Come, get up, why are you sleeping so late?' demanded Nastasia, as she entered the room. She was a strong young country girl who cooked and cleaned for the whole house. 'Sit up. I've brought you some soup. You look very pale. Don't you eat anything these days?' She sat beside Raskolnikoff on his sofa while he ate. 'Prascovia Paulovna is going to report you to the police.'

'Why? What have I done?' the young man asked.

'You don't pay your rent, and you won't give up this room. A landlady must make money from her rooms. She wants you out.'

'I'll talk to her tomorrow.'

'But tell me, Rodion Romanovitch,' Nastasia said, 'why do you, who are so intelligent, lie here doing nothing? You used to go to the university, and you used to give lessons, but now you don't work and have no money.'

'I have thinking to do,' the young man replied very seriously.

'And does your thinking bring you any money?'

'I hate teaching, and I can only make a few kopecks from it, which isn't worth my time,' answered Raskolnikoff.

'Oh, so you are thinking of ways to make a great fortune?'

'Yes, a fortune,' answered Raskolnikoff mysteriously.

'You frighten me. You look terrible and you sound crazy. Oh, I almost forgot, a letter came for you this morning. Here it is.'

Raskolnikoff went very white as he took the letter and saw that it was from his dear mother. He had received nothing from her in more than two months. 'Go, Nastasia. I need to be alone.'

The envelope trembled in Raskolnikoff's fingers as he put it to his lips and kissed it before nervously opening it. It read:

Please forgive me for my long silence, my dear Rodion, and remember that your sister Dounia and I love you more than life itself. All our hopes and dreams depend completely on your future success and happiness. It broke my heart to learn that you had abandoned your university studies because of lack of money. Until now we could do so little to help you, but that may change very soon.

First, you must know that Dounia has been living with me for the last six weeks. She was forced to leave her position as governess with the Svidrigaïloff family because the master of the house tried to take advantage of her. She did everything she could to keep him away, but one day his wife heard him trying to persuade Dounia to leave the country with him. Mrs Svidrigaïloff was certain that your sister was as guilty as her husband and immediately threw her out of the house.

That was not the end of it. The woman went from house to house telling people that Dounia was dishonest and immoral. Our neighbours stopped speaking to us, and I considered leaving this town, but Dounia was strong and comforted me.

But do not worry – through God's mercy our troubles came to an end. Mr Svidrigaïloff finally told his wife the truth, showing her a letter in which Dounia had refused his invitations and offers of love. Mrs Svidrigaïloff came straight to us and begged to be forgiven. Then she returned to every house in town and announced Dounia's innocence. Dounia was offered several teaching positions with good families.

But Dounia will not be working as a governess in future. You see, dearest Rodion, your sister has received and accepted an offer of marriage from a distant relative of Mrs Svidrigaïloff's. It was this dear lady who introduced us to Peter Petrovitch Looshin, a successful lawyer. He is respectable, with a solid character and a secure future, and although at forty-five he is much older than Dounia, he is still good-looking and can be charming. He wants a wife who has known poverty and misfortune so that she will always be grateful to him.

I must admit that he did not impress me at first – he was very proud, even rude. But Dounia is happy to make her life with him, although she cannot love him. She says he is an honourable man who will provide for all three of us, and her plan is to persuade Peter Petrovitch to give you a good job after we move to St Petersburg, which we will do very soon. But at present your sister will not talk to her future husband about you because he wants to form his own judgement when he meets you.

So now we are preparing to travel to St Petersburg. Peter Petrovitch will go ahead of us and find a place for us to stay until the marriage. You, Dounia and I will be together again after a separation of nearly three years. Dounia is wild with joy at the idea of seeing you and joked once that she would marry Peter Petrovitch for that alone.

I was able to borrow against my pension, so I am sending you a little money – thirty-five roubles. I wish it were more, but you will understand that we need a certain amount for our travelling expenses and for our rooms when we arrive. Peter Petrovitch will arrange the transportation of our luggage.

Now that you know our story, I must finish. My dearest son, I send you a mother's love and prayers. Do you still trust in God's love and mercy? Do you remember kneeling beside your father when you were a child, praying to God, our Father in Heaven? How happy we all were then!

Until we meet – very soon – I am yours, while life lasts,
Pulcheria Raskolnikoff

Raskolnikoff's face was wet with tears, but there was a bitter smile on his lips. He felt he could not breathe in his filthy little room and, grabbing his hat, ran down the stairs. As he hurried along the crowded streets, he talked to himself, giving the impression of a madman or a drunkard.

'This marriage will never take place while I'm alive. This Mr Looshin and his desire for a poor, grateful wife can go to the devil! No, Dounia!' he shouted, almost spitting out his words as he marched along. 'You will not accept this sensible, business-like lawyer – with his fortune – as your husband.

'How could my mother let her sweet daughter sacrifice herself for my benefit and marry without love? How could she approve of a man who allows her to borrow against her small pension to pay for her own transport to St Petersburg?

'Dounia is a strong girl with a strict character. She fought off Mr Svidrigaïloff, and she suffered the false accusations of her neighbours. She would never sell herself to any man for her own benefit, but she would make this sacrifice for someone she loves – for a mother, for a brother, she would sacrifice all.

'Does she not see that her situation is worse than Sonia's? Marmeladoff's daughter has no choice – she must sell her body or watch her family starve. My sister isn't starving, she can find a position, she can reject Mr Looshin. You will not do this for me, Dounia. Never, while I live.'

Raskolnikoff's thoughts troubled him. Although it was always at the back of his mind, he had ignored his mother's and sister's situation for too long. 'I must act now or give up life completely!' he cried with great excitement. Marmeladoff's question from the night before came back to him: 'What can a person do if he has nowhere to go?'

'Where am I going?' Raskolnikoff said aloud, looking round for the first time since leaving his room. 'I'll go to see Razoumikhin. He might be able to help me get some translation work, or perhaps he could lend me a little money for new boots and a jacket so I'm fit to give lessons again.'

Raskolnikoff had had very few friends at the university. The other students considered him serious, intellectual and proud; although they respected him, they avoided him. But Razoumikhin – generous, kind and fun-loving – had declared himself to be Raskolnikoff's friend. He too was very poor; but unlike Raskolnikoff he approached life with a positive attitude, working hard both at his studies and at teaching and always glad to see his rather difficult companion.

But as usual, Raskolnikoff could not make up his mind. 'It's a crazy idea to visit Razoumikhin,' he said to himself. And then, a moment later, a new idea occurred to him: 'Yes, I will go to him, but not now. I'll visit him the day after *that*, when my new life has begun – but will *that* ever really happen?'

Raskolnikoff walked on without any destination in mind, and at sunset, having walked aimlessly for several hours, he was surprised to find himself in the Haymarket. He was a very superstitious young man and in the future would examine these days and believe that his actions had been determined by a force greater than himself. 'What has brought me to this particular place at this time of evening?' he wondered.

As he crossed the square, careful to attract no one's attention, the traders were packing up their goods and closing their stalls for the night. At the far corner Raskolnikoff noticed Elizabeth Ivanovna, the younger sister of the old moneylender, talking to two of the traders. Elizabeth was a tall, awkward woman, about thirty-five years old, shy and quiet, not very intelligent, and a slave to her sister, who beat her when she did not work hard enough. At this moment she looked nervous and confused.

'Decide for yourself, Elizabeth Ivanovna,' said the man. 'Come tomorrow at seven. There's a foreign family who need to sell some of their things. Maybe you can help them.'

'Tomorrow?' asked Elizabeth slowly, as if she could not imagine doing anything so daring.

'You're like a child,' the man's wife said. 'Alena Ivanovna is just your stepsister. Don't let her give you orders all the time.'

'Come without asking her,' interrupted the man. 'Be here at seven o'clock tomorrow evening. OK?'

'Yes, I'll come,' agreed Elizabeth shyly, before saying good night and leaving the Haymarket.

Raskolnikoff walked away, too, with a feeling of actual terror. He had learned by accident that Alena Ivanovna would be alone in her flat the next evening at seven o'clock. His chance arrival in the Haymarket had stolen his freedom to make his own decisions; everything had been decided for him. There would never be a more convenient time to return to the moneylender's flat. In this period of his life every circumstance, like hearing Elizabeth's plans for the next evening, seemed to him to contribute in some mysterious way to his fate.

For example, in the previous winter on his first visit to Alena Ivanovna's flat, for no apparent reason he had felt an immediate hatred for the miserable old witch. He had left her flat with two roubles for a pawned ring and stopped at a cheap café for a pot of tea. He did not believe it was an accident that two other students had been sitting at the next table, talking about the old moneylender.

'She's useful to all of us because we need money from time to time,' began the first student, 'but her interest rates are unfair, and she sells people's precious things if they're one day late with the money they owe her. I've heard that she has a fortune hidden in her flat, and when she dies it will all go to the church. The priests will be paid to pray for her soul, and her sweet, obedient sister, who she treats like a slave, will get nothing. Why should Alena Ivanovna live for no purpose? Why should her gold be used to protect her evil soul? Her money could save her sister as well as dozens of families from poverty, crime and ruin.'

'What are you suggesting?' asked his friend.

'Kill her and use her riches for the good the poor. Wouldn't the murder of one worthless old woman be excused, even approved of, if it made possible a thousand good deeds? Of course I wouldn't kill Alena Ivanovna *myself*. It would require a stronger man than I am to rid society of this wicked creature.'

As the two students left, Raskolnikoff wondered if there was a reason why he had heard this insignificant conversation. The ideas were not new or revolutionary, but they seemed to be aimed directly at him since he had just left Alena Ivanovna's flat. The students had planted an idea in his brain and from that moment he began to see himself as the instrument of a fixed purpose.

♦

Raskolnikoff woke at twelve the day after his visit to the market, when Nastasia brought him a bowl of soup. After letting the rest of the afternoon slip away as he lay on his little sofa, dreaming of distant lands, he was shocked to hear the clock in the square strike six, which meant that he must get busy if he wanted to complete his task.

His first job was to sew a piece of cloth into the inside of his coat to make a secret place to hang a hatchet and carry it unnoticed through the streets.

Next, he removed a small package from its hiding place under his floor. This was actually a smooth piece of wood wrapped in paper and tied tightly with string, but he hoped the moneylender would believe it was the silver cigarette case he had promised to bring to her. Then he heard someone in the street below shout, 'Come in now! It's past seven o'clock.'

'Past seven! It can't be!' thought Raskolnikoff. He hurried out of his room and crept down the stairs as quietly as a cat. He planned to steal the hatchet that was kept in the kitchen, but Nastasia, who was usually out of the house at this hour, was washing clothes. Though she looked up and saw him, he hurried on without speaking to her.

He now felt totally defeated and unsure of what to do, but when he reached the yard he noticed something shiny in the corner of the old porter's hut. No one was near, and when he called for the porter there was no answer. He rushed into the hut and saw it was a hatchet under the old man's workbench. Without hesitating he hung the tool on the cloth he had sewn inside his coat and made his way out into the street.

'There's more of the devil than my design in all this,' he thought, smiling to himself. The convenient position of the hatchet had given him new courage and strengthened his conviction that his plan was worthwhile.

It was half-past seven by the time he entered the building where Alena Ivanovna lived. His heart was beating rapidly as he climbed the stairs, listening for any unusual sounds. Fortunately the stairs were empty and every door except one was closed. The open door was to an empty flat on the second floor where two painters were working. They did not look up from their tasks as Raskolnikoff crept past.

At last he reached the moneylender's door. The flat opposite was still unoccupied and apparently the flat below was empty, too, since the name card on the door had gone. 'Shouldn't I leave now?' the young man asked himself, but instead of leaving he waited and listened. Silence.

He touched the hatchet, took a deep breath and rang Alena Ivanovna's bell. After waiting half a minute, he rang again – this time a little louder. No answer. No sound except the pounding of his heart. The old woman was always at home, but today she was likely to be more suspicious than usual because she was alone. He sensed her presence on the other side of the door and moved around rather noisily to remove any mystery from the situation. He rang the bell a third time, gently and politely, without giving the smallest sign of impatience. Then he heard Alena Ivanovna unbolt the door.

As before, the door was opened a little and Raskolnikoff could see the old woman's suspicious eyes staring out at him. Losing his self-control, he frightened Alena Ivanovna and caused her to lose her balance by pulling the door open. He pushed past her and entered the room without her permission.

The old woman followed and recognized him when she saw him in the light. 'What do you want now? What's your name again?'

'Pardon me, Alena Ivanovna. You remember – I'm Rodion Raskolnikoff. I have something to pawn, a silver cigarette case, as I promised the other day. Please, have a look at it.'

Before taking the package, the moneylender inspected the young man. 'Why are you so pale? Why are your hands shaking?'

'Fever,' replied Raskolnikoff shortly. 'You'd be pale too if you had nothing to eat.'

The old woman accepted this explanation and took the package. 'What a tight knot you've put in this string!' she complained, turning towards the light from the window.

With her back to him, Raskolnikoff opened his jacket and removed the hatchet. His arms felt weak and stiff.

'What's this? A piece of wood?' cried Alena Ivanovna as she angrily turned to face him.

There was no time to lose. Raskolnikoff raised the hatchet with both hands and let it descend without force, almost mechanically, on the old woman's head. With the faintest of cries, she fell in a heap to the floor, but still with the strength to raise her arms to the wound. Seeing this, Raskolnikoff, with increased force, struck twice more with the hatchet until blood flowed freely from her head. He saw that her neck was broken and her skull crushed, and had no doubt that she was dead.

The murderer, calm and businesslike, began searching the dead body. He found a thick piece of string – now wet with blood – around her neck, and attached to this a small purse full of money and two crosses, one made of cheap metal and the other of wood. He cut the string with his hatchet and, after finding the old woman's keys in her pocket, went to the bedroom. Stopping in the middle of the room, he considered turning around and leaving the flat immediately but smiled at the thought, knowing it was too late now.

Under the old woman's bed he found a large trunk and, inside it, all sorts of jewellery: watches, bracelets, chains, earrings. He was putting these things into his jacket pockets when he heard footsteps in the other room. He froze with terror, listened, not daring to breathe, and heard a soft cry.

Raskolnikoff picked up the hatchet and rushed out of the bedroom. In the other room he saw Elizabeth standing beside her sister's bloody body, too frightened to make another sound. The murderer did not hesitate but ran at the woman and with one heavy blow split her skull in two. Elizabeth fell down dead.

Now Raskolnikoff was in a state of shock, overcome by the thought of the horrible crimes he had committed. Nothing could make him return to the bedroom; he had no thought of gold or cash – he stood there, fixed to the floor, in a kind of dream. Glancing into the kitchen after a time, he noticed a bucket of water, and spent more than five minutes washing the blood from his hands and wiping it from the hatchet and his boots.

He stopped and looked round the tiny room. 'What am I doing? Am I going mad? I must get away from here at once!'

He passed the bodies and stepped outside. Down below, probably at the street door, he could hear two men arguing. He waited patiently, and at last they left the building. Then he heard someone leave another flat, whistling as he descended the stairs. Finally there was silence and he closed the door behind him and prepared to make his escape.

Suddenly he became aware of a new sound: footsteps at the bottom, but rising slowly and steadily. He was sure that someone was coming *there*, to the old woman's place on the fourth floor. He heard the man coming closer but he could not move a muscle.

Just as the man reached the bottom of the last set of stairs, Raskolnikoff came alive and hurried back into Alena Ivanovna's flat, very quietly closing the door and bolting it. By that time the visitor had reached the door and rang the bell noisily. The man waited a few seconds and rang again. Losing patience, he began to shake the door and to shout, 'Are you asleep or has someone killed you? Alena Ivanovna, you old witch, open this door!'

The visitor was still shouting and ringing the bell when another man arrived. 'Is it possible there's no one at home?' the latter, a much younger man, asked.

'Who knows? I've almost broken the lock with my pounding. The old witch is always here.'

'Wait!' the younger man shouted. 'Look at the door. It resists when I pull on it.'

'So what?'

'The door isn't locked, it's bolted. To bolt one's door, one must be at home. Don't you understand?'

'You're right! But why doesn't anyone open the door?'

'There's something peculiar about this,' the younger man said. 'We should get the porter up here. He can break down the door and find out what's happened.'

Both men started down the stairs. 'Stay here by the door,' shouted the younger man. 'I'll run down and get the porter.'

Left alone, the older man continued to knock, ring the bell and shake the door handle. All this time, Raskolnikoff stood on the other side of the door with the hatchet in his hands. He was in a state of nervous excitement, waiting to attack the men if they forced their way into the flat. Then he heard the man on the other side of the door begin to curse. 'The devil take her! She can go to hell!' Obviously tired of waiting, he went down the stairs to find the younger man.

Raskolnikoff slid the bolt across and silently opened the door. He listened to the man descending the stairs and then heard voices at the bottom. Almost immediately three men began to climb the stairs; no longer hoping to escape, Raskolnikoff decided to go out and meet them. But on the second floor, just before he ran into the men, he saw the open door to the flat where the painters had been working earlier. Creeping into the empty room and hiding behind the door, he was just in time to hear the three men hurry past, on their way to the fourth floor. He heard them disappear into the flat, and then he hurried down the stairs as fast as his trembling legs would carry him.

No one on the stairs. No one at the door. He walked into the street as slowly as he could and disappeared into the crowd. Great drops of sweat ran down his face as he imagined the three men discovering the dead bodies in a pool of blood, but no one took any notice of him.

Though he could hardly walk, Raskolnikoff soon found himself at his own building and, for the first time, wondered what to do with the hatchet. As before, he believed that something or someone was guiding his actions. The porter's door was closed but not locked, so he opened it and, without thinking, walked into the empty hut and returned the hatchet to its exact place under the workbench.

He reached his room without meeting anyone and threw himself on his sofa just as he was. He did not sleep but lay there almost unconscious, his head swimming with terrible thoughts that he could make no sense of.

Chapter 2   Fever

At two o'clock in the morning Raskolnikoff was woken from a feverish sleep by the sound of drunkards being thrown out of the taverns. He sat up quickly and looked round his cheerless little room in confusion, as the events of the previous evening came flooding back to him. He opened his door and listened; all was silence in the house.

He had lain on his bed since the night before, having neither removed his clothes nor bolted his door. Shaking with cold, he now took his clothes off to examine them for clues to his crime. He found a few drops of dried blood along the ends of his trouser legs and cut off the edges of the cloth with his knife.

For the first time he thought of the old woman's purse and jewellery, hidden in the pockets of his jacket. How could he have forgotten these things, even when he was searching his clothes for evidence of the crime? He quickly emptied his pockets and put everything into a hole in the wall behind a loose piece of wallpaper.

'There, it's out of sight!' he thought with relief, but then he looked at the lump in the wall and was filled with terror. 'What's the matter with me? Is that the way to hide stolen goods? I must really be going mad. What else should I do?'

He thought of the cloth he had sewn inside his jacket for transporting the hatchet, tore it out and cut it into small pieces. Looking again at his clothes, he found blood on the lining of his jacket, in his pockets and on his boots. He cleaned his boots and then removed the lining and pockets from his jacket but could not decide how to get rid of them.

'What am I doing?' he asked himself again and again. 'Can this be my punishment beginning already?'

But instead of taking action, he fell back on to his sofa and into a deep sleep, holding the bloody rags tightly to his chest.

Hours later he heard Nastasia at his door. 'Open the door, Raskolnikoff,' she shouted. 'Don't lie there like a dog. It's eleven o'clock in the morning and the porter is here with a summons from the police for you.'

'They know everything,' thought Raskolnikoff, as he struggled to his feet and unbolted the door.

'Here's your summons,' said the porter, taking a long, suspicious look at Raskolnikoff. 'You must report to the police station.'

'What for?' asked the young man, taking the summons in one trembling hand while holding the bloody rags in the other.

'What's that in your hand?' Nastasia asked.

Raskolnikoff quickly hid the rags under his pillow and turned to the two visitors. 'Please leave. I must get ready to go to the police station at once.'

When they were gone, he began to prepare himself to confess his crimes.

He left his apartment building in a state of anxiety, which was made worse by the terrible heat and the crowds of people on the street. 'Why have the police summoned me? Have they found something that links me with the two murders? Why don't I go in, fall on my knees and confess everything? Surely that would end my suffering.'

These thoughts ran through his head as he made his way unsteadily to the second floor of the police station. He felt ill again and was almost overcome by the powerful smell of fresh paint coming from somewhere in the building.

When he reached the required office, Raskolnikoff walked up to the clerk at the reception desk and asked rudely, 'What do you want from me?'

The clerk glanced at the summons and told Raskolnikoff to take a seat with the others waiting to be interviewed. The young man began to relax because the clerk had not paid him any special attention. Perhaps there was a simple explanation for being called to the police station. 'How stupid of me!' he thought. 'He knows nothing. I was thinking of confessing for no reason.'

After a while, Raskolnikoff approached the desk again. 'Excuse me, I've already been here for more than a quarter of an hour.'

'Don't complain, young man,' said the clerk. 'Sit down and keep silent until you're called.'

'Why should I stay silent?' asked Raskolnikoff. 'I have a right to question why I've been summoned.'

The clerk looked at Raskolnikoff's summons again. 'Complaints have been made against you. You're required to pay 120 roubles in rent which you owe to your landlady, Prascovia Paulovna. When do you intend to pay this debt?'

Smiling to himself, Raskolnikoff felt safe again, knowing that no one suspected him of anything more than a minor debt. 'I can't pay at present. I have no money and no job. I've had to give up my studies at the university because I'm so poor, but my situation may change soon.'

A senior officer had walked into the office and stood listening to the exchange between the clerk and Raskolnikoff.

'There are complaints against you. You must pay or give up the room,' shouted the clerk.

'Poverty is no crime,' said the senior officer, whose name was Nicodemus Thomich. His polite manner and kind words impressed Raskolnikoff.

'Thank you, sir,' Raskolnikoff began. 'I'm a poor student – at least I was until I ran out of money – in bad health because I rarely have enough to eat. You may judge for yourself whether or not I can pay this debt today. My mother and sister will send me something soon, and then I will give Prascovia Paulovna what I owe her.'

'We're not interested in your mother and sister,' interrupted the clerk. 'You'll have to sign a promise that you'll pay your rent by the end of the year. Now sit down and I'll tell you what to write.' The young clerk began and Raskolnikoff tried to write what he said, but the pen fell from his fingers.

'You're ill, aren't you?' Nicodemus Thomich commented. 'You've written enough. Just sign the paper and you can go.'

Raskolnikoff was exhausted and sat down again with his head in his hands. Once more he considered confessing his crimes, feeling that Nicodemus Thomich would listen to him and perhaps even understand his actions. But then he heard the officer and the clerk discussing something else – something that caught his attention.

'I don't think they're guilty,' said the officer. 'The porter saw them both enter the building, and then they came down to ask him to open Alena Ivanovna's door. They weren't trying to get away from the scene of the crime.'

'But they said the door was bolted,' added the clerk, 'and when they returned to the fourth floor with the porter, the door was open and there was no one inside, just two dead bodies.'

'Did no one see someone running out of the building with blood on his hands?' asked the clerk.

'Nobody noticed anything, but how could they?' responded Nicodemus Thomich. 'That building is full of all sorts of people coming and going throughout the day and night. A dozen murderers could have escaped unnoticed.'

Raskolnikoff picked up his hat and started towards the door, but the next thing he was aware of was sitting on a hard chair while a junior clerk offered him a glass of yellowish water.

Nicodemus Thomich was standing in front of him, searching his face. 'Have you been ill very long? You couldn't hold the pen for more than a few seconds and now you've fainted.'

'I've had a fever since yesterday,' Raskolnikoff replied.

'Go home when you're ready,' Nicodemus Thomich said.

The office was silent when Raskolnikoff left, but as he walked down the stairs he could hear a lively discussion begin again. By the time he reached the street he was certain that they knew something. 'I bet they're going to search my room. They suspect me, I'm sure of it.' Fear possessed him from head to foot, and he felt the fever return as he made his way home.

When he reached his room, he rushed to the obvious lump in the wallpaper and removed all of Alena Ivanovna's things. With the purse and the various pieces of jewellery hidden in his trouser pockets, he hurried out of his room again, certain that the police would arrive at any moment.

'I'll throw everything into the river,' he thought as he pushed through the crowds on the pavement, but when he arrived there he had second thoughts. 'Someone will see me here, and some of the little boxes may not sink. I'll bury everything in the forest – but I must hurry. The police might be searching for me now.'

As Raskolnikoff turned a corner onto a quieter street, he changed his plans again when he saw a ruined building sitting in a courtyard. There was a lot of rubbish along one side of the building and a hut, perhaps the workshop of a carpenter or a bricklayer. He spied a large rock, weighing about twenty-five kilograms, resting beside one wall of the building.

'This is the perfect spot,' he thought. 'No one's around and no one can see me from any windows or from the street.' With a great effort, he managed to turn the rock over and found a shallow hole underneath it. Quickly throwing everything into the hole, he finally managed to move the rock back into place.

'Perfect!' he laughed, as he went back to the busy street. 'The evidence is buried, I'm a free man.'

Suddenly a new, urgent question came into Raskolnikoff's head and spoiled his good mood. 'Did I murder Alena Ivanovna with a definite goal in mind, or was it simply a senseless act? I wanted to throw everything into the river – so what was it all for? I'm ill and tired . . . I'll be better soon . . . Everything will make sense then.'

He kept on walking, hoping to clear his mind, and found himself near Dmitri Prokovitch Razoumikhin's lodgings. 'I think Razoumikhin lives in that house. How strange! I said I would visit him *afterwards*, and here I am.'

He walked up to the fifth floor and knocked on his friend's door. Razoumikhin was astonished to see Raskolnikoff after an absence of more than four months. 'Impossible!' he cried. 'How wonderful to see you! Come in, come in!' But he saw immediately that something was wrong. 'Are you all right? You're so thin. Are you ill?'

'No, of course not. I'm here – that's all, but if you're going to bother me with questions, I'll leave at once.'

'No, I won't let you go like this. I have some translation work which I can share with you. Will you let me help you a little?'

'You're the kindest, wisest man I know, but there's nothing I want from you,' whispered Raskolnikoff in a voice full of pain.

Raskolnikoff's surprise visit and his strange attitude puzzled Razoumikhin. 'You must have a fever. Where are you living now? I'll take you home.'

Raskolnikoff did not answer but simply turned his back and left, as if he had again isolated himself from everything and everybody. Back in his room after wandering the streets for hours, he once again fainted on his little sofa.

♦

Raskolnikoff remained on his bed with a fever for four days, but he was not alone, as he might have wished. Nastasia and his true friend, Razoumikhin, who had followed him from his own house, sat with him as he suffered from bad dreams and frightening visions. Razoumikhin brought his friend Dr Zosimoff to him twice, and Nastasia gave him a little cold tea whenever she could. Finally one morning at ten o'clock, Raskolnikoff opened his eyes and knew where he was. He recognized his friend and Nastasia, but looked in the corner and saw an office clerk who was a stranger to him.

'Who's that, Nastasia?' he asked, pointing at the man.

'I'm here from the bank,' the man answered himself. 'I've been instructed to give you thirty-five roubles, sent to you from your mother, Pulcheria Alexandrovna. Will you please sign my book as a receipt?'

'I don't want it,' Raskolnikoff said, pushing the book away.

'Not want it?' asked Razoumikhin. 'It'll allow you to eat and to buy new clothes. Here, I'll guide your hand.' He helped Raskolnikoff to sign the book and sent the clerk away. 'Now you must eat. Nastasia, can you bring us some food?'

Razoumikhin helped Raskolnikoff with his soup and spoke to him gently. 'You mustn't worry any longer. I've been to the police station and had a word with Nicodemus Thomich, who has torn up the promise you signed because your landlady, dear Mrs Paulovna, said she was content to trust you for the rent.' Raskolnikoff remained silent. 'Don't be angry. You were very ill, and I wanted to help.'

'Did I know you when I had the fever? Did I make any sense when I spoke?' asked Raskolnikoff.

'Sometimes I couldn't understand what you were talking about – something about earrings and a gold chain, and you kept asking about your boots. You spoke also of Nicodemus Thomich and the smell of paint at the police station. But forget all that. You're well now, and we have business to talk about. Here's your thirty-five roubles. I'm going to take ten and get you some new clothes.'

As soon as the door was closed, Raskolnikoff leapt out of bed and looked wildly round the room. 'My God, my God, tell me, please: Do they know everything or nothing?' He checked the hole behind the wallpaper and found nothing. He looked at his boots and found that they were covered in mud with no sign of blood, but still he could not calm down.

'I must leave at once, but where can I go? Maybe to America.'

But instead of escaping, he fell on to his little sofa again and was soon deep in sleep.

Six hours later, Razoumikhin returned with Dr Zosimoff and gently woke Raskolnikoff. 'You look better, my friend,' began Razoumikhin. 'The food and sleep have been good for you. And look, I've brought you a new cap, trousers, three shirts, a jacket and boots. None of it's new, but everything is fairly good quality, and all of it cost just nine roubles and fifty-five kopecks. You'll look very smart in these things. Try them on.'

'How did you pay for all of this? Where did the money come from?' Raskolnikoff asked suspiciously.

'The money? It's yours – from your mother. Don't you remember this morning?' Razoumikhin reminded him.

'I remember now,' Raskolnikoff admitted after a long, uncomfortable silence.

'Good,' commented the young doctor. 'And how do you feel?'

'I'm quite well, but I don't want to try on new clothes,' replied Raskolnikoff rudely. He stared at Dr Zosimoff and tried to raise himself off the sofa, but he was too weak and fell back again into his old position, with his face turned towards the wall.

'I was thinking about taking him to my house this evening. It's very near here, and he could lie quietly on the sofa. I thought it would do him good to be in society,' suggested Razoumikhin.

'I don't think you should move him yet. Look, he's asleep again already,' Zosimoff said.

'I'll do whatever you instruct, but listen, I hope you'll come this evening. A few interesting people will be there: some people from the university and Porphyrius Petrovitch – he's a magistrate in this district and a relative of mine. He knows everything about the investigation into the murder of that old moneylender and her sister. One of the painters who was in the building at the time has been charged with the murders,' reported Razoumikhin.

'What kind of proof do they have?' asked Dr Zosimoff.

'None. Porphyrius Petrovitch hinted that he thinks they're on a false track, just as they were when they questioned the two men who discovered the bodies, Koch and Pestryakoff. There was no evidence linking them to the murders, and the same is true of this painter, Nikola. The only fact against him is that on the night of the murders he got very drunk after finishing work, and didn't arrive at work the next morning. He can't account for his movements, so of course this makes him guilty in the eyes of the police.'

'Perhaps they think he was spending Alena Ivanovna's money in the taverns,' said the young doctor.

'More than ten people have reported to the police that they saw Nikola and Dmitri, the other painter, leave the building on the night of the murders – several of them talked and joked with the men. A minute or two later, Koch and Pestryakoff were looking for the porter, asking for help to open Alena Ivanovna's bolted door. Don't you see? First, the painters couldn't be behind the bolted door and in the yard talking to neighbours at the same time. And, second, the murderer must have seized his one opportunity to escape.'

'How?' asked the doctor.

'By leaving Alena Ivanovna's apartment when Koch and Pestryakoff were both downstairs, then hiding in the empty room where the painters had been working and escaping when Koch, Petryakoff and the porter went back to the fourth floor.'

'It's almost like a play at the theatre,' Dr Zosimoff said. 'My guess is that she was killed by one of her debtors; money is always a motive.'

'I agree, and so does Porphyrius Petrovitch, who's investigating all Alena Ivanovna's clients.'

'Her clients?' Raskolnikoff asked suddenly. Obviously he had been listening closely to the whole conversation. 'How does your relative know who they are?'

'Their names were written on the things they'd pawned. The murderer was better at killing than at stealing – he took very little: ten or twenty roubles and a few bits of jewellery. The police found a lot more gold and jewellery, more than 1,500 roubles in cash and a fortune in bank cheques still hidden around the apartment.'

'What else do the police say?' Raskolnikoff asked, his voice trembling with excitement and fear. But the discussion was interrupted by a knock at the door.

The visitor walked in without being invited, although he was a stranger to the three men. He looked boldly round the low dark room and did not try to hide his disgust at everything he saw, including the sight of Raskolnikoff lying undressed and unwashed on his miserable, filthy sofa.

He turned his back on Raskolnikoff and addressed Dr Zosimoff, the most respectable-looking of the three young men: 'I wish to see Rodion Romanovitch Raskolnikoff, a student. Is he here?'

'That's him,' the young doctor replied, nodding towards the bed.

Raskolnikoff sat up and, in a weak voice, said, 'I'm Raskolnikoff. What do you want?'

The visitor examined him and replied, 'I am Peter Petrovitch Looshin. My name is familiar to you, I assume.'

Instead of answering, Raskolnikoff lay back on his sofa and stared at the ceiling.

'Don't take offence,' Razoumikhin said to the visitor. 'You see, Rodion has been ill for the last five days, and for three he didn't even know where he was, but he's better now. I'm his friend, and this gentleman is the doctor who's been looking after him. And now, sir, will you please say what your business is?'

Looshin turned his attention back to Raskolnikoff. 'I believe that your mother has written to you about me.'

'Oh, you must be the bridegroom. Yes, I know about you. I know too much,' said Raskolnikoff, staring directly at Looshin.

In fact, Peter Petrovitch Looshin looked like a bridegroom on this summer afternoon. His clothes were very smart, but perhaps too new for this occasion. With his elegant hat, fine leather gloves and bright tie, he looked like a model in a shop window.

After another uncomfortable silence, Looshin apparently decided to take no notice of the impolite treatment he was receiving. 'If I'd known about your illness, Rodion Romanovitch, I would have visited you earlier, but I've been busy at the law court and have been preparing for the arrival of your mother and sister. I've found rooms for them near here, in Bakalieff's house.'

'That's a horrible place − filthy and full of criminals,' Razoumikhin interrupted. 'However, it is cheap.'

'I don't know St Petersburg very well, but the two rooms for Pulcheria Alexandrovna and her daughter are clean, and I'm preparing a house that will be ready for the day I marry Dounia.' He turned towards Raskolnikoff. 'I can see that you're not well. I hope to know you better when you're fully recovered.'

Raskolnikoff did not reply, and Looshin rose from his chair, but before he could depart Raskolnikoff shouted angrily, 'But is it the truth?' His face had a wild look of joy at giving offence to this man. 'Is it true that you told your future bride that you chose her because she was poor and you could dominate her easily, and because she would always be grateful to you for saving her from poverty?'

'Sir,' replied Looshin, blushing with annoyance, 'you have been given entirely the wrong interpretation of my motives, I suspect by your mother. She's a woman of superior character, but I'm amazed that she could believe . . .'

'Stop!' screamed Raskolnikoff. 'If you breathe one more word against my mother, I'll throw you down the stairs.'

'I've been tolerant until now, but I won't be threatened with violence,' Looshin said, turning pale and biting his lip, trying to hide his emotion. 'I have been tolerant of your unfriendly attitude since I arrived at your lodgings and I have stayed here in order to discover the cause. I was ready to forgive your rudeness because you're ill, but . . .'

'I'm not ill!' cried Raskolnikoff. 'Now go to the devil!'

Looshin left the room without uttering another word.

'Leave me! Leave me, both of you!' Raskolnikoff shouted at his friends. 'I don't fear you! Let me be alone! Alone! Alone!'

'Let's go,' Dr Zosimoff said to Razoumikhin. 'We mustn't upset him more.' On the way down the stairs, he continued, 'There's something on his mind, something that's a heavy burden to him, I fear.'

'It must be his sister's engagement to that fool, Peter Petrovitch,' Razoumikhin said.

'Maybe that's the problem, but he was also upset when we were talking about the murders,' added the doctor.

'You're right. And apparently he fainted at the police station when the same subject was mentioned,' said Razoumikhin.

'I'll check on him in a short time – I'm sure we'll find a way to help him get better,' Zosimoff said.

When his friends had gone, Raskolnikoff bolted his door and dressed himself in the clothes that Razoumikhin had purchased for him. He felt an unexpected calm in his mind; there was not a trace of fever now, nor any feeling of terror. He had decided to finish everything today. Although he was not sure how he would do this, he knew that this evening would bring the situation to an end. He picked up the twenty-five roubles, with the change that Razoumikhin had left, and went out into the street in the direction of the Haymarket, thinking about life and death.

'I once read about a man who had been sentenced to death, and when the time came he said he would live alone on a high, narrow rock in endless storms and darkness if he could live. Just live, no matter how, just live. Oh God, how true! I want to live!'

An hour later Raskolnikoff was leaving a café where he had stopped for tea and to read the newspapers when he found himself face-to-face with Razoumikhin.

'Rodion, what are you doing here? You should be at home in bed. Explain yourself,' Razoumikhin lectured his friend.

'I was tired of you. You worry too much about me. I want to be alone, please get away from me,' Raskolnikoff said as he tried to push past his friend. 'I don't want your kindness.'

'My dear brother, I want to help you, so I'll leave you in peace, but please come to my flat this evening. Being with others will help you forget whatever's troubling you.'

'I won't come, Razoumikhin,' replied Raskolnikoff. 'Now please let me pass.'

The two young men went their separate ways – Razoumikhin to his flat to prepare for his guests, and Raskolnikoff to the bridge over the River Neva. His depressed mood had returned and he stared at the water. His eyes saw blood, he felt faint, and everything – houses, people, carriages – went round and round.

'Not water – that won't solve my problem,' he said aloud, dismissing the idea of suicide by drowning. But he wondered what had happened to his earlier decision to end it all. 'Oh, how tired I feel. My illness has come back, and I wish I could lie down.'

But instead of going directly back to his room, Raskolnikoff wandered from street to street with his eyes fixed on the ground. Then, as if a voice had whispered in his ear, he looked up and saw that he was in front of Alena Ivanovna's building. As quick as lightning, an idea rushed into his head and he climbed the dark stairs to the old moneylender's flat. The door was wide open and he could hear voices inside; two workmen were hanging new wallpaper. Raskolnikoff walked in and stood beside the window in the sitting room.

'What do you want here?' asked one of the workmen.

Instead of answering, Raskolnikoff walked to the outer door and pulled on the bell. He pulled again and again as he stood there listening and thinking.

'Hey, stop that!' shouted the workman. 'What are you doing?'

'I want to rent some rooms,' said Raskolnikoff.

'That's not our business. Go and talk to the porter.'

'In the morning!' added the other workman. 'People don't rent rooms at nine o'clock at night.'

Raskolnikoff ignored their comments and stared at the floor. 'Where's the blood? The old woman's and her sister's? There was a lot of blood, a pool of it.'

'Come on, we're finished for the night. It's time you left,' said Aleshka, the first workman, nervously.

When the three men reached the ground floor, they saw the porter. 'This young man came upstairs to look at the rooms we were working in,' Aleshka explained. 'He wanted to know what had happened to all the blood.'

'Who are you?' the porter asked impatiently. 'What were you doing in those rooms?'

'I'm Rodion Romanovitch Raskolnikoff, ex-student, and I live near here. Why shouldn't I look at some empty rooms?'

'Out you go, you're wasting my time,' said the porter as he pushed Raskolnikoff into the street.

'What shall I do now?' thought Raskolnikoff, as he picked himself up and walked back over the bridge. He repeated to himself that his suffering would soon be at an end because he had decided to go to the police and confess, but suddenly his thoughts were disturbed by screaming and shouting.

He rushed to join the crowd surrounding a gentleman's carriage, pushed his way to the front and saw the cause of the excitement: a man of about fifty lay on the street, with blood streaming from his face on to his dirty clothes. He had fallen under the carriage and been crushed by the horses' feet.

'I was driving very carefully, with my light on,' insisted the driver to the policemen, who had just arrived. 'I saw this fellow on the pavement and shouted at him to keep back, but he stepped directly in front of me. I tried to stop, but it was too late – the horses couldn't avoid him.'

People in the crowd agreed with the coachman's story, shouting: 'Quite right, we saw it all.' 'The man is drunk – it's his own fault.'

The police were preparing to carry the injured man to hospital when Raskolnikoff recognized him. 'I know him! I know him!' he cried, pushing right to the front. 'His name's Marmeladoff – he lives very near here. Call for a doctor, quick. I'll pay!'

The police were happy to hand over responsibility for Marmeladoff to Raskolnikoff, especially since he kept repeating, 'I'll pay.' With the help of three other men, he was soon carrying Marmeladoff up the stairs and into Catherine Ivanovna's miserable room.

'What are you bringing here? Oh, my God in heaven, what's this disaster?' cried Catherine. She stood very straight and deadly pale, breathing with great difficulty. The children screamed and held on to their mother's skirt when they saw the injured man.

With Marmeladoff on the only bed in the room, Catherine pushed her children to one side and began to nurse her husband. As she placed a pillow under his head, unbuttoned his shirt and removed his tie, she remained calm and efficient.

'I've sent for a doctor,' Raskolnikoff told Catherine. 'Don't worry, I'm going to pay. He'll be all right, you'll see.' Then with a towel and basin of water, she began to wipe the blood from Marmeladoff's face and from his crushed chest.

'Polenka!' Catherine Ivanovna shouted at her eldest child, 'run quickly and find Sonia. Tell her that her father has been run over and needs her at once.' She could say no more because she began coughing violently.

Her attention then returned to her husband, who had regained consciousness and was trying to speak. He struggled to get air, while large drops of sweat stood out on his forehead and blood ran from his mouth and chest.

'My God! Look at his poor chest! Look at the blood!' screamed Catherine, desperate with fear for her husband's life.

Marmeladoff recognized his wife and managed to whisper, 'A priest!' Then he saw the two youngest children and said, 'The poor, hungry children.'

'Silence!' shouted Catherine Ivanovna. 'You ought to know why they're hungry.'

Finally the doctor arrived, but after a brief examination of the patient, he turned to Catherine and said, 'His chest and throat are very badly injured. He'll be dead in five minutes.'

As the doctor left, an old grey-haired priest pushed through the crowd of neighbours filling the hall. All of them, including Peter Petrovitch Looshin, who had recently moved into the building, were attracted by the possibility of witnessing a death. When the priest knelt beside Marmeladoff's bed, Raskolnikoff, the family and the neighbours fell to their knees and remained silent as the priest performed the ceremony for the dying.

Just as he finished, Polenka and an older girl arrived at the door. Sonia, Marmeladoff's only child, made her way shyly to her father's side. Like most of the people in the room, she was dressed in cheap clothes, but hers were noticeable because they were the usual costume of a prostitute: a silk dress in bright colours, a few feathers, some cheap jewellery and a fancy little umbrella, which was completely unnecessary in July.

The priest wanted to leave, but Catherine Ivanovna grabbed his arm and asked, 'What will happen to my children now?'

'Pray to God for his help and mercy, madam. Trust in him and he will take care of you,' the priest began.

'God doesn't help people like us. Our lives were ruined by this man, always drinking, robbing my children of food and clothes. I thank God that he's dying – no one will miss him.'

'Madam, you should forgive in the hour of death. It's wicked to have such thoughts,' lectured the priest.

Ignoring the priest and his empty words, Catherine Ivanovna turned to her husband and wiped the sweat from his face and smoothed his pillow. She began coughing again and put a handkerchief to her mouth. When she showed him the blood she had coughed up, the priest quietly hurried from the room.

Marmeladoff, now in terrible pain, stared at his wife but could not speak. 'Don't talk,' Catherine said to him gently. 'I know what you want to say. I pardon you – now rest peacefully.'

Then the dying man saw his daughter, Sonia, standing beside the bed. 'Who are you?' he whispered. He had never seen her in her working costume, but suddenly he recognized her. 'Sonia, my daughter! Forgive me!' The young girl knelt beside her father's bed and held him in her arms, where he died.

'How will I bury him?' cried Catherine Ivanovna as she stared at her husband's body. 'How will I feed my children?'

Raskolnikoff, full of pity for the young widow, said, 'Catherine Ivanovna, I met your husband last week and heard the story of his life. He loved and respected you and, in spite of his weakness for drink, he cared for nothing more than his family. Please allow me to help you, for his sake, with these twenty roubles, and I'll come again, perhaps, tomorrow. For now, I'll say goodbye.'

Raskolnikoff left immediately, hurrying past Mr Looshin without seeing him at the back of the crowd of neighbours. On the stairs he came face-to-face with Nicodemus Thomich, the senior officer he had met at the police station. The two men recognized each other at once.

'Marmeladoff is dead,' Raskolnikoff reported. 'A doctor and a priest both visited him, so all is in order. You're a kind man, sir. I hope you can comfort his widow.'

Thomich looked closely at Raskolnikoff. 'You're wet with blood,' he said.

'Yes, I'm covered in blood,' Raskolnikoff answered mysteriously, smiling as he continued down the stairs, but he was stopped once more before he reached the bottom.

'Sir! Sir!' shouted Polenka from above him. 'Please tell us your name. My mother and Sonia want to thank you.'

'You don't need to thank me, but will you pray for me? My name is Rodion Romanovitch Raskolnikoff.'

'Yes, sir, our father who has just died taught us to pray. Now I will pray for him and for you every night before I go to sleep.' She threw her arms around his neck and kissed his cheek before returning to her mother and Sonia.

Alone on the street, Raskolnikoff said to himself, 'That's enough. Now I must rid myself of ghosts and fear, because I intend to live this life. I feel weak in my body, but my soul is strong and I must live. I didn't die with that old woman.'

While his good mood lasted, Raskolnikoff turned in the direction of Razoumikhin's flat and soon found himself at a party with about twenty-five other guests. Razoumikhin, who had been drinking freely for a couple of hours, was very glad to see his friend. 'Welcome, Rodion, please come in and have something to eat and drink.'

'I've only come to give you my best wishes and to thank you for being such a kind friend,' began Raskolnikoff. 'I'm feeling very weak again and will go home now.'

'I'll accompany you to your house,' said Razoumikhin. 'My guests won't miss me for fifteen minutes.'

As they walked along, Razoumikhin chatted a little drunkenly. 'I'm sorry you couldn't come in and meet my uncle, Porphyrius Petrovitch. He's a dear old fellow, and he's read an article you wrote for a law journal. He wants to meet you to talk about your theories on crime. Dr Zosimoff's at the party, too. Do you know that yesterday he said he thought you might be going mad? And the clerk from the police station told us that you'd fainted when you were there. What was that about?'

'There was no air in the office, and I could smell paint.'

'I think it was your fever, too,' added Razoumikhin.

'Listen, Razoumikhin, I've just watched a man die, and I've given his widow most of my money, and I've met his daughter – a wonderful, beautiful girl who if I'd killed anyone . . . oh, I'm stupid. Hold my arm, I may faint again. I'm full of sorrow for the widow and her children, and my head is spinning. Please help me to my room.'

As the two young men approached the room, they heard voices. Raskolnikoff threw the door open and, seeing his mother and sister sitting on his filthy sofa, fainted once again.

Chapter 3   Suffering

When he regained consciousness, the look on Raskolnikoff's face – something between sorrow and anxiety – frightened both his mother, Pulcheria Alexandrovna, and his sister, Dounia Romanovna. Their concern for their son and brother grew even greater when he pointed at Razoumikhn and said, 'He can take you to your rooms. I don't want to see you today.'

'But Rodion,' Pulcheria Alexandrovna began, 'we've just arrived. Can't I stay with you for a single moment after being separated from you for three years?'

'We should go,' whispered Dounia. 'We're upsetting him.'

'Just one thing before you go, Dounia,' Raskolnikoff said. 'You should know that I've seen Looshin. I won't allow you to marry this man on my behalf. I might already be ruined, but there's no reason why you should be crushed by that fool. If you marry him, I'll no longer call you my sister. You must choose between Looshin and me. And now, please get out of my sight.'

'Rodion, have you lost your mind?' shouted Razoumikhin. 'You can't speak to your sister in this way.'

'Please,' begged Raskolnikoff, 'please, take them away.' He fell on to his sofa and turned his face to the wall.

Razoumikhin immediately led the ladies out of the room, and though they were nervous about trusting this slightly drunk stranger, they could see that he had looked after Raskolnikoff as a true friend. Anyway, it was late and they were unfamiliar with St Petersburg.

'You mustn't worry about Rodion,' Razoumikhin explained. 'I'll go back to him after I see you to your lodgings, and I'll take Dr Zosimoff with me. If his condition gets worse during the night, I promise that I'll come back for you at once.'

And with those words, Razoumikhin fell to his knees in the street and kissed the hands of Pulcheria Alexandrovna and her daughter. 'You're the fountain of goodness and reason and perfection. I've had a lot of wine tonight, but I know what I am saying: you ladies have set my heart on fire.'

'Please, sir, get up. You're embarrassing us,' Dounia said, feeling quite alarmed by Razoumikhin's emotional little speech.

'I beg your pardon, but you're perfect!' replied the young man as he got to his feet. 'Look. Here's your building, and Mr Looshin deserves to be whipped for putting you here. What sort of man is your future husband?'

'Mr Razoumikhin, you seem to forget who you're talking about,' began Pulcheria Alexandrovna.

'You're absolutely right. Please accept my apology, but here are your rooms. Rodion's illness was very severe, and for a time the doctor even wondered if he was going mad. He still needs a lot of sleep in order to recover completely, but with the doctor's care I'm sure he'll be greatly improved by the morning. But now, please go to bed at once – you too need your rest. Remember to lock your door after I leave. I'll bring you news in the morning.'

As he returned to Raskolnikoff, determined to watch him with even gentler care, Razoumikhin thought about the two women. The mother was still beautiful at forty-three, although her hair had begun to turn grey and lines had gathered at the corners of her eyes. She was naturally shy and affectionate but not weak; she would always stand firm if her principles were questioned. Dounia, on the other hand, was very young – only nineteen, in fact – but she had the intelligence and grace of an older woman. She was tall and beautiful with brown hair, dark eyes like her brother's and a look that was both sweet and proud. Razoumikhin had never seen anyone so handsome and so charming – for him it was love at first sight, and would have been even without the wine.

♦

The following morning, soon after seven o'clock, Razoumikhin awoke from a troubled sleep with his head full of worries. How drunk had he been on the previous night? What had he told Raskolnikoff's mother and sister about his sick friend's mental condition? Why had he questioned Looshin's reputation? And why had he been so bold and open about his feelings towards Pulcheria Alexandrovna's daughter?

Although these questions made him quite nervous about how the ladies would greet him, he dressed carefully and arrived at their rooms exactly at nine o'clock. He received a warm welcome, which pleased him even more than it surprised him.

They invited him to join them for breakfast at their humble table.

Throughout the meal, which lasted almost forty-five minutes, the women asked a steady stream of questions about their favourite subject: Raskolnikoff. Razoumikhin kept his answers positive, but at the same time he tried to give a fair idea of the problems which Raskolnikoff had been facing.

'Lately Rodion has changed, spending more and more time alone in his room. I think there are two sides to his personality. He's kind and generous, but prefers to hide these qualities and appear cruel. He's also suspicious and cold and rejects friendship and society, but I'm sure that your arrival will bring him back to good health, both mentally and physically. Soon he'll be the old Rodion that you both love so well.'

'May I ask another question?' Pulcheria Alexandrovna requested.

'Of course. For you, anything.'

'We find ourselves in a difficult situation,' the older woman began. 'Early this morning we received a letter from Peter Petrovitch Looshin, making his excuses for failing to meet us at the station yesterday. Dounia's future husband writes that he will visit us here at eight o'clock this evening, but he warns us that he won't meet with us if my son is here because Rodion insulted him so rudely. He also adds that it's his duty to tell us that he saw my son in the rooms of a drunkard who died yesterday. Rodion, according to Peter Petrovitch, gave twenty roubles from my pension to the dead man's daughter, a prostitute, although he pretended to give the money to the man's widow for funeral expenses. Now what should I do? Should I believe these stories and forbid my son to come here?'

'Have faith in Rodion,' suggested Razoumikhin. 'He loves you both with all his heart. He wasn't himself yesterday, but I'm sure he'll receive you warmly today.'

Pulcheria Alexandrovna and the two young people were greeted at the door of Raskolnikoff's room by Dr Zosimoff, who had just examined his patient. 'Ladies, you'll be astonished by the change in your dear son and brother. You can see that in three or four days he will have completely recovered.'

'Doctor, I must thank you for the excellent treatment you have given my son. Both you and your friend have helped him through this difficult time,' said Raskolnikoff's mother.

'Mother, please let me apologize to you for last night. I didn't intend to keep you waiting and then to treat you like strangers.' Raskolnikoff said these kind words in a cold, unfeeling voice, but he turned and held out his hand to Dounia, giving her an affectionate, brotherly look. Dounia seized his hand with joy and grasped it warmly to her heart. Pulcheria Alexandrovna observed this gesture, which showed that her children had reached an understanding, and she was filled with love for them.

'I wanted to come to your rooms early this morning, Mother, but my clothes were covered in blood,' Raskolnikoff said.

'Blood! What blood?' asked Pulcheria Alexandrovna in alarm.

'Please don't worry. I wasn't injured, Mother, but while I was walking aimlessly through the streets yesterday afternoon, feeling confused because of my fever, I found a man I slightly knew crushed under the wheels of a carriage. I don't know why, but I helped carry the man home – getting blood on my clothes in the process – and paid for a doctor to come.

'I must have been going mad because of the fever, but after the man died, I did something that was unforgivable: I gave almost all the money you sent me to the widow to pay for the funeral. The woman was coughing blood and trying to comfort her three small children, but they have no money and no way to get any unless the woman's stepdaughter brings her a few kopecks when she sells herself on the street. If you'd seen the miserable room and the hungry children, you might have given them the money too, but I had no right to give away what you'd sacrificed so much to give me.'

'Rodion, you mustn't blame yourself,' replied his mother. 'I have no doubt you always act for the best.'

'Don't be so sure of that,' he replied with a bitter smile.

'My son, my only need is to be with you again.'

'Say no more, Mother,' whispered Raskolnikoff, becoming excited and nervous, but holding his mother's hand. 'We'll have plenty of time to talk later.' But Raskolnikoff did not believe his own words because he planned to isolate himself from everyone, including his mother and sister. This goal suddenly became so clear in his mind that he stood up and started towards the door.

'Where are you going?' Razoumikhin asked, grabbing him by the arm.

Raskolnikoff sat down again without a word, but shocked his family and friends even more by suddenly shouting, 'How dull you all are! Can't you think of anything to talk about?'

'What's the matter with you, Rodion?' asked Dounia anxiously. 'You're frightening us.'

'Forgive me,' Raskolnikoff said. 'It was just some nonsense that came into my head, but I'm all right now.' He rose and kissed his mother before sitting down again.

'Rodion, this room is so small – it's like living in a grave. I'm sure it's made you depressed and has caused your fever.'

'This room? I think what you say is true, Mother.' Then he became silent again, feeling impatient towards his mother and sister. But suddenly he remembered what he needed to say: 'Listen, Dounia, I apologize for my behaviour yesterday but I haven't changed my opinion of Looshin. If you marry him, I'll cease to consider you my sister.'

'My dear brother,' answered Dounia, 'you imagine that I'm sacrificing myself for you, but you're mistaken. I've accepted

Peter Petrovitch because he's offered me a better life, and I intend to be the kind of good and loyal wife he expects.'

'You'll do whatever he expects?'

'Yes, up to a certain point, but I won't marry him unless I'm sure that I can respect him thoroughly. But even if you were right, and I were marrying this man to help you, what would my sin be? If I'm injuring anyone, it's only myself – I'm not guilty of murder. Why are you looking at me like that, Rodion? Why are you so pale?'

'It's nothing – I'm all right now.'

'Please, Rodion, read this letter which Peter Petrovitch sent us this morning,' said Dounia.

Raskolnikoff read the letter through twice carefully, and then handed it back to his sister. The others waited nervously for an explosion of anger, but he remained calm. 'I understand from this that if you don't obey him, and you let me come to your rooms, he'll end your engagement and abandon you completely.'

'That seems to be what he's saying,' agreed Dounia.

'He also tells you that I gave the money from Mother to the dead man's daughter, a prostitute. I've already told you that twenty roubles went to the widow for funeral expenses. I'd never met the daughter until I saw the man die in her arms. Mr Looshin's goal is clear – he wants to make you question my behaviour and to separate us. This letter reveals his dishonest character – and there's little sign of any feeling for you. What shall I do this evening, dear sister?'

'I must have you beside me at this meeting, Rodion,' said Dounia. 'I beg you and your friend, Dmitri, to come.'

'We'll join you without fail this evening at eight o'clock,' said Raskolnikoff.

Just at this moment, when Raskolnikoff, his mother and his sister began to feel like one family again, the door opened silently and a girl entered the room, looking shyly around at each face. At first Raskolnikoff did not recognize Sonia Semenovna Marmeladoff because today she was dressed very simply, like a respectable but poor teenage girl. Seeing so many people in the room, she became nervous and confused, but Raskolnikoff spoke to her kindly. 'Sonia Semenovna, come in. I didn't expect to see you here. Please take a seat.'

Sonia sat down but was greatly embarrassed because she knew that it was not acceptable for her, a prostitute, to sit down in the same room as two respectable ladies. Feeling very nervous, she stood up again, looked at Raskolnikoff and said softly, 'Catherine Ivanovna has sent me to beg you to honour us by coming to the funeral service for my father tomorrow at St Mitrophane's Church, and afterwards back to the room where my father died for a dinner.'

'I'll certainly try to be there,' said Raskolnikoff. 'Are you in a hurry? I'm anxious to have a word with you.'

The young girl looked amazed at this suggestion, but she was too afraid to excuse herself. 'My stepmother also requested me to thank you for the help you gave us yesterday. Without you we couldn't give my father a decent funeral.'

'Mother,' Raskolnikoff said, 'this is Sonia Semenovna, the daughter of Mr Marmeladoff, who was run over yesterday.' As he spoke, Raskolnikoff examined Sonia carefully and took note of her thin, pale face, her small nose and chin and her beautiful blue eyes, which gave her whole face a kind, friendly look.

Pulcheria Alexandrovna and Dounia Romanovna did not greet Sonia because they knew her by reputation.

Raskolnikoff kept his eyes on Sonia and hurried on, 'I see you're looking at my room. My mother said it's like a grave.'

'But yesterday you gave us all your money,' Sonia replied, looking as if she was ready to cry. From the first moment in the room, she had been upset by the poverty in which Raskolnikoff lived. There was a silence, but now both of the other women were looking at Sonia more sympathetically.

Pulcheria Alexandrovna broke the silence by rising and saying, 'Rodion, we will leave now so that you can have a rest, but we expect you and Dmitri Prokovitch to dine with us before our meeting with Peter Petrovitch Looshin.' Having said this, she hurried out of the room, but her daughter surprised everyone by stopping in front of Sonia and bowing very politely to her. Before she could follow her mother out the door, Raskolnikoff took his sister's hand and a happy look of understanding passed from brother to sister and back again.

'That's how things should be,' said Raskolnikoff, looking almost cheerful for a change as he returned to Sonia. 'Before our chat, will you please excuse me for a minute or two so that I can have a word with Razoumikhin?' He turned towards his old friend. 'You know Porphyrius Petrovitch, don't you?'

'Of course I do. I've told you – he's a relative of mine. Why do you ask?'

'I heard you say that he's questioning clients of the moneylender who was murdered recently.'

'Yes, that's true. What about it?'

'I pawned a couple things with Alena Ivanovna – in total not worth more than five or six roubles – but they're important to me. One was a ring Dounia gave me before I went to university, and the other was my father's silver watch, the only thing I have left of him, so I'd hate to lose it forever.'

'You must speak to Porphyrius Petrovitch. We can go to his house at once, it's very close to here.'

Moving towards the door, Raskolnikoff spoke to his other visitor. 'Sonia Semenovna, this is my friend Razoumikhin, a good fellow. Can you leave with us now and allow me to visit you later today?'

Sonia was more embarrassed than ever, but gave Raskolnikoff her address and left the building with the two young men. 'Goodbye, Mr Raskolnikoff, and thank you. I'll tell Catherine Ivanovna to expect you tomorrow.'

She hurried off, staring at the pavement as she thought about her extraordinary visit to Raskolnikoff's room and about the fact that he would visit her later that day. In fact, her mind was so busy with these thoughts that she did not notice that a stranger had been following her since she left Raskolnikoff's building. This stranger looked much younger than his fifty years. His clothes were elegant and everything else about him — from his neat beard to his expensive shoes — indicated that he was a rich gentleman. He had been passing when he heard Sonia's words, 'Goodbye, Mr Raskolnikoff . . .' and carefully but quickly, he looked at the three young people and at the building behind them. Then he followed Sonia, feeling certain that he had seen her somewhere before. The mystery of Sonia's identity was eventually solved because she entered the same building in which the stranger was staying. The gentleman saw that they lived on the same floor and were, in fact, next-door neighbours.

Razoumikhin was in an excellent mood as he and Raskolnikoff turned in the opposite direction from Sonia, heading for Porphyrius Petrovitch's office. 'Rodion, I didn't know that you'd pawned things with that old woman. Is it long since you saw her?'

'I think it was about two days before she was killed. Why?'

'When you were ill with the fever, you talked about rings and watch chains, and now I understand why.'

Raskolnikoff, wondering if Razoumikhin had been suspicious of his feverish talk about jewellery, changed the subject and asked, 'What kind of man is Porphyrius Petrovitch?'

'He's a great man — one of the best, as you will see. He can be awkward because he's very intelligent — like you — and he enjoys playing with people and keeping them guessing about his motives. He's a famous lawyer and has solved some very tricky cases. I think you'll find him unusual and interesting, and he definitely wants to meet you.'

'Why would he want to meet me?'

'Well, when you were ill he heard Zosimoff and me talking about you. He was sorry to hear you'd given up your law studies at the university, and he'd hoped to meet you at my little party last night. Look, here's the place – he has his office and his apartment in this building.'

As they approached the building, Raskolnikoff thought about Porphyrius Petrovitch. 'Does he know that I returned to the murder scene yesterday and asked about the blood in Alena Ivanovna's flat? I must find out.' Then, turning to Razoumikhin, he said aloud, 'You've been in a good mood all day, and you blushed when my mother invited you to dine with us this evening.'

'You're imagining things!' shouted Razoumikhin.

'You're blushing now. Why have you dressed so carefully and put oil on your hair? Is it for my sister?'

'Oh, please shut up! You're horrible!'

Raskolnikoff burst out laughing and, as he had planned, was still laughing when the two young men walked into Porphyrius Petrovitch's apartment. He wanted the famous magistrate to see two good friends enjoying themselves.

'Please don't let me interrupt your joke,' said Porphyrius Petrovitch as he waited for the two young men to calm down.

'No more nonsense!' said Razoumikhin, looking seriously at Raskolnikoff. Then, turning to Porphyrius Petrovitch, he said, 'Permit me to introduce to you my friend Rodion Romanovitch Raskolnikoff, who has a little affair to discuss with you.'

Porphyrius Petrovitch was dressed informally for such an important legal expert, but this was his home as well as his office.

He was about thirty-five years old with light hair and yellowish skin and neither a beard nor a moustache. He gave the impression of an active, cheerful and highly intelligent man. He politely invited his guests to sit down and gave Raskolnikoff his full attention before giving his opinion. 'You must write a statement, telling the police that certain articles found in Alena Ivanovna's flat are yours, and that you wish to claim them.'

'Unfortunately, I don't have the money to claim them now, but I wish to make it clear that the items are mine. They're not worth much money, but the silver watch is all my father left me, and my mother would be very upset if she knew I no longer possessed it.' All the time he was speaking, Raskolnikoff was wondering how he appeared to Porphyrius Petrovitch. Did he sound truthful and sincere? Did he seem nervous?

'You don't need to pay for your pawned items at this time. They'll be kept for you,' the magistrate said calmly. 'Do you know, I've been expecting your visit for some time.'

'Really?' asked Razoumikhin. 'But how did you know he'd pawned anything with the old woman?'

Looking directly at Raskolnikoff, Porphyrius Petrovitch replied, 'Your ring and watch were at Alena Ivanovna's flat, wrapped in paper with your name and the date she'd received them written clearly on the packages. Nearly everyone who had items with the old moneylender has already been to the police to claim their things. You're almost the last one.'

'What a memory you must have!' said Raskolnikoff, with an insincere smile, but trying to meet the lawyer's stare and to sound unworried. However, he added in a shaky voice, 'I've been rather ill lately.'

'Yes, I've heard about your fever, and even now you're pale.'

'I'm not pale. I'm very well, in fact,' Raskolnikoff insisted, but he heard his voice becoming angry, even violent. He told himself to stay unemotional or he would say something stupid.

'Very *well*! That's crazy!' said Razoumikhin. 'Until yesterday he could hardly stand up, but when Dr Zosimoff left him alone, he dressed and walked the streets until midnight.' Then he turned to Raskolnikoff and asked, 'Why did you go out? Zosimoff and I thought you'd gone completely mad.'

Raskolnikoff ignored Razoumikhin and addressed himself to Porphyrius Petrovitch, saying, 'I went out in search of a new place to live, somewhere private and away from people like my friend here and that doctor, who want to disturb my peace.'

'Interesting,' commented Porphyrius Petrovitch coolly. 'This morning Nicodemus Thomich told me that he met you late last night in the room of a minor government official who'd been run over and killed by a carriage.'

'Exactly!' shouted Razoumikhin. 'You went there and gave the widow all your money. Wasn't that the action of a very sick, possibly mad man?'

'Perhaps I found a jewel there,' Raskolnikoff said before turning to Porphyrius Petrovitch again, and in a nervous voice saying, 'I apologize for taking so much of your time.'

'No apologies are necessary! I'm delighted by your visit, and now I'm going to order some tea, and then we'll continue this entertaining conversation.'

While Porphyrius Petrovitch was out of the room, Raskolnikoff considered the magistrate's attitude towards him. 'He's very clever, playing with me like a cat with a mouse. Why does he already know so much about me – where I've been and what I've done and who I've talked to since the murder? He's fishing for facts, but the truth is he has no evidence to link me to the murder, so I must be cautious and take care with what I say.'

As Porphyrius Petrovitch came back into the room, Raskolnikoff turned to Razoumikhin and said cheerfully, 'Was your party a success? There seemed to be a lot of lively conversation going on.'

'I think the discussion would have interested you. The question was, "Does crime exist?" – and my guests found a lot of nonsense to say on that topic,' reported Razoumikhin. 'The argument centred on the theory that crime is a protest against a badly-organized society. Man, therefore, is driven to commit crimes for environmental reasons and no other.'

'Talking of crime and environment,' began Porphyrius Petrovitch, looking at Raskolnikoff, 'I was delighted to read an article of yours in a law journal. I congratulate you on a very interesting, important piece of work about the psychological condition of a criminal when he commits his deed – that he is always, more or less, mentally unbalanced.'

'Thank you, sir. I must admit I didn't know the article had been published, but I remember it well,' Raskolnikoff said.

'I was especially interested in your idea, at the end of the article, that there are men who have an absolute right to commit all kinds of wicked acts, men for whom laws don't exist. You described two categories of men: ordinary men who must be obedient and follow the laws of the land, and extraordinary men who have a right to commit every kind of crime and break every law because of their superior character. Am I right in thinking that's what you meant?'

'Almost, but you imply that extraordinary men should commit criminal acts at all times, which was not my meaning. My theory is that an extraordinary man can be guided by his conscience, even if that means breaking the law and committing a criminal act. He may do this in order to benefit mankind.

'Think about this: all great rulers have been criminals because they have created new laws which have forced them to break the old ones. In consequence, all men who want to achieve something new, something extraordinary, must be willing to commit crimes in order to overcome any barriers that might be in their path.

'Nature divides men into two categories: the first is ordinary, inferior men who are born to produce children, to love and to obey and follow the laws of the land. The second class of men, however, consists of extraordinary men who destroy what exists in order to create something that *should* exist. While carrying out their plans for a new society, these extraordinary men have the right to commit crimes, to murder and even to start wars – but only if these acts lead to something better for mankind.

'Society needs both categories of man – one to produce children and to maintain ordinary life, and the other to excite mankind and to make people act for change. Unfortunately, there are very few men who are born with new ideas – perhaps one in a thousand has an independent mind, maybe one in a million is a true master, and probably one in thousands of millions can change the world.'

'Rodion,' Razoumikhin interrupted, 'I'm very upset by the idea that some men have a moral right to murder. To me, this seems worse than allowing a government to have that right.'

'I agree,' added Porphyrius Petrovitch. 'In fact, I think it's much worse. For example, if a young man sees himself as a great leader with big ideas, his first step will be to destroy every barrier that stands in his way, which means stealing to get money and murdering to get rid of his enemies.'

'But society has laws,' said Raskolnikoff, 'and the police will catch this imaginary man and stop him – and even if he's clever enough to avoid capture, he'll have to live with his own conscience. He'll know that he's sinned and will pity his victims. He'll suffer from guilt and doubts, but he'll have to live with this suffering in order to achieve his goals.'

'Please, excuse me . . . I hardly know how to ask my question – a psychological one,' Porphyrius Petrovitch said with hesitation. 'While you were writing your article, am I right to think that you saw yourself as one of those *extraordinary* men?'

'Very likely,' answered Raskolnikoff in a challenging tone.

'So I can assume that to assist mankind, you'd be willing to break down barriers, for instance to kill and to rob?' Porphyrius asked, laughing silently.

'If I intended to do anything like that, I certainly wouldn't tell you,' answered Raskolnikoff, looking directly at the magistrate.

'A theoretical question only, I assure you,' Porphyrius Petrovitch replied, 'to understand your article more clearly.'

Raskolnikoff looked at the lawyer with disgust and thought, 'What an obvious trap!' and then said, 'I'm neither a great political nor religious leader, nor anything like that; therefore, I can't imagine what I'd do if I were one.'

In the silence that followed, Raskolnikoff simply stared at Porphyrius Petrovitch and prepared to depart.

'Are you leaving so soon?' the magistrate asked, offering Raskolnikoff his hand to shake. 'I'm delighted to have met you, and if you come again tomorrow I'll help you with your letter to the police about your pawned possessions. We'll have a chat about Alena Ivanovna, too, since you were one of the last people to see her alive.'

'Are you suggesting a formal interview?' asked Raskolnikoff.

'You misunderstand me – I've had a chat with everyone who had recently pawned items with the old woman. I've managed to find out some valuable bits of information. Oh, I almost forgot, on the evening when you went to Alena Ivanovna's flat, was it between seven and eight that you rang her bell?'

'Yes,' replied Raskolnikoff.

'And as you went up to the fourth floor, you must have seen two painters working in a flat on the second floor. Is that right?'

'Painters? No, I didn't see any painters,' Raskolnikoff answered slowly, as if he was checking his memory of that day, but really taking care to avoid Porphyrius Petrovitch's trap. 'I did see some porters moving a sofa from the second flat on the fourth floor – but no painters.'

'What are you talking about?' interrupted Razoumikhin excitedly. 'The painters were in the flat on the second floor on the day of the murder, not on the day of Rodion's visit.'

'I beg your pardon, I've mixed up the dates,' cried Porphyrius Petrovitch, tapping his forehead and smiling as he showed his visitors to the door.

The two friends remained silent as they walked along the street, each analysing what Porphyrius Petrovitch had said. Finally Razoumikhin exploded excitedly, 'How dare he ask questions that imply you know something about those murders!'

'I've thought about every word spoken by Porphyrius Petrovitch. He tried to trap me, but he has no evidence to link me to those murders, only suspicions. I'm sure he has his own system for solving cases, but I'm not going to let his questioning upset me.'

'But I can see how you became a suspect: a poor, desperate student, suffering from poverty and illness, but confident in his superior intelligence and worth, becomes seriously depressed after isolating himself in a miserable room for six months. You went to the police station because you hadn't paid your rent, dressed in rags, hungry and ill. The crowd of people in the airless office and the smell of paint overcame you, and you fainted. Because of all this, you became a suspect in a murder case. It's ridiculous!'

As they walked along, Raskolnikoff thought about his friend's analysis of Porphyrius Petrovitch's reasoning, but just as they reached the door of his mother's and sister's lodgings, he was seized with a sudden anxiety which he could not control.

'Go in without me, please, Razoumikhin. I must be alone. I'll return in half an hour,' and Raskolnikoff hurried off in the direction of his own room. He needed to assure himself that he had moved all Alena Ivanovna's money and bits and pieces of jewellery from the hiding place behind the loose wallpaper. Greatly relieved at finding nothing when he searched the hiding place, he took his cap and quietly left his room, but he was stopped by the porter at the entrance gate.

'Here he is now,' the porter shouted at a poor, sad-looking little man of about fifty. 'This is the student, Raskolnikoff.'

The individual standing with the porter looked at Raskolnikoff out of the corner of his eye, examining him slowly and silently, and then moved away from the building.

'What's that about?' Raskolnikoff asked the porter.

'I have no idea,' answered the porter. 'He came here asking for you by name, but he didn't say what he wanted.'

Raskolnikoff followed the stranger and soon caught up with him. 'You asked for me at the porter's. What do you want?'

The man raised his eyes and stared at the young man with a threatening look. 'Murderer!' he whispered, quietly but distinctly.

Raskolnikoff's heart pounded violently, his legs shook and a cold sweat poured down his cheeks. 'What do you – how? – *who* is a murderer?' he asked in a trembling voice.

'It's you! *You're* a murderer!' said the little man with a smile full of hatred on his lips. Then he turned at the next corner, leaving Raskolnikoff thoroughly frightened.

Raskolnikoff made his way back to his room, forgetting about his mother and sister, and lay motionless and confused on his little sofa, trying to make sense of what he had just experienced on the street. 'Who was that man? Is it possible that he could have seen everything? But how? And why didn't he accuse me before today? Why did I ever think that killing an old moneylender, someone no better than a louse, would achieve anything? This act was neither noble nor extraordinary. It meant nothing. But if she came to life again, I would kill her again – but not Elizabeth.

Elizabeth! Sonia! Poor, gentle creatures who accept their fate in silence!'

Raskolnikoff's thoughts exhausted him, and he finally fell into a deep sleep and dreamed that he was once again following his accuser, trying to get through the crowds of people on his way to Alena Ivanovna's flat. When the two men reached the building, the little man disappeared and Raskolnikoff climbed the dark stairs on his own, passing the painters on the second floor before entering the flat on the fourth floor.

Everything was as it had been on the night of the murders, except that Alena Ivanovna was sitting silently in her chair near the window. Raskolnikoff lifted his hatchet and struck her skull twice, but the old woman, laughing silently, did not move and did not bleed. With the power of the devil, Raskolnikoff struck again and again, but the old woman refused to die. He wanted to run away, but the hallway and the stairs were crowded with people who watched him in silence. His own scream woke him, and he sat up covered in sweat.

Chapter 4   Madness

When Raskolnikoff finally came to his senses, he looked up and saw a man he had never seen before watching him from his doorway. The stranger came into the room, softly closed the door behind him, sat down at the table and stared at Raskolnikoff without saying a word. Finally the young man could not bear the silence and said, 'Why don't you speak? What do you want from me?'

'Permit me to introduce myself: I am Arcadius Ivanovitch Svidrigaïloff. I think you know that my name has been connected to your sister's in the past, and I'm here because of her.'

'Svidrigaïloff? Nonsense! It isn't possible,' Raskolnikoff said after more silence. 'What are you doing here?'

'I've come for two reasons: first, I wanted to meet you, having heard so many impressive stories about you. And second, I thought you'd listen to what I have to say and then persuade your sister to see me.'

Raskolnikoff stared at his visitor and again remained silent, so Svidrigaïloff continued, 'I didn't harm your sister. I simply fell in love with her, and I always admired and respected her. My feelings for her were genuine, but those days have passed. I'm here, not to declare my love for Dounia Romanovna, but to tell her that my wife, Marfa Petrovna, has died and has left 3,000 roubles for her.'

'How did your wife die?' Raskolnikoff asked rather rudely.

'Oh, are you suspicious of me? You wouldn't be the only one. There were silly rumours flying around that I had something to do with her death, but the police and the medical experts agree that she wasn't murdered but died of a heart attack after too much food and wine, followed by a very hot bath. My conscience is clear. Marfa Petrovna was very fond of me, rescuing me from terrible debts by marrying me, and we were happy for seven years. We hardly ever quarrelled, and I used the whip on her only three times.'

'Are you fond of using a whip on ladies?' Raskolnikoff asked.

'Not particularly, but I think my wife rather liked the excitement the whip caused. Judge me for yourself – I think you'll find me a civilized man and not some sort of devil.'

'I still don't understand why you're here.'

'I can do what I like. My wife has left me plenty of money, but I'm tired of most entertainment. I've already seen Europe, I'm sick of card games and even drink, which used to be my comfort but now makes me ill,' explained Svidrigaïloff.

'It seems that your wife's death has left a hole in your life.'

'Perhaps, but I haven't lost her completely because her ghost speaks to me about everyday concerns: asking for my opinion of her dress, for example.'

'And what do you tell her?' asked Raskolnikoff.

'The last time, I told her I planned to re-marry very soon, and with that news she disappeared.'

'Perhaps you should see a doctor,' suggested Raskolnikoff.

'I know perfectly well that I'm ill, but to tell the truth I don't know what's the matter with me. Is it necessary, as some people say, to be sick in order to see ghosts? Do you ever see them?' Svidrigaïloff asked.

'No, because they don't exist,' insisted Raskolnikoff.

'But if there's another life, a next world, a person's illness can bring him closer to that other world,' Svidrigaïloff continued.

'I don't believe in another world,' Raskolnikoff said, 'and I must go out, so please explain to me the purpose of your visit.'

'Yes, of course. I think your sister plans to marry Peter Petrovitch Looshin. If you've met him, you'll know that he isn't suitable for her, and that she'd only marry him to save her family. I loved your sister once because she's not only young and beautiful, but also kind, generous and intelligent, but I'm not a serious man and my love for her has ended. Nevertheless, I want to organize my affairs, so I've left my children, who are now very rich and independent, with their aunts, and I want to stop Dounia Romanovna from marrying this ridiculous man. If you'd kindly set up a meeting between her and me, I'd beg her to forgive me, and I'd ask her to accept 10,000 roubles from me to make up for any troubles I've caused her.'

'You're mad! How dare you speak in this way about my sister!' Raskolnikoff cried.

'Stop and think,' begged Svidrigaïloff. 'My offer is unselfish and honest; I don't want anything in return. In fact, I may marry soon and will never see Dounia Romanovna again. But I think you understand that if she doesn't take *my* money, she'll have to take money from Mr Looshin and for that, there will be conditions. Let me help her.'

'She'll never accept your money,' insisted Raskolnikoff.

'Why not let *her* decide that? Get me a private interview with her, that's all I ask. And, when you speak to her, please tell her that Marfa Petrovna has left her 3,000 roubles.'

'Is that true?' asked Raskolnikoff.

'My dear fellow, why can't you trust me? Can't you see we have a lot in common? Of course it's true, so tell her soon. I'll contact you – I'm staying in a flat quite near here.'

As Svidrigaïloff left, he passed Razoumikhin on the stairs, and the young man asked Raskolnokoff, 'Who was that?'

'Svidrigaïloff, the landowner who almost ruined Dounia's reputation. I don't trust him, so can I ask you to promise to protect my sister from him?'

'Yes, that's something I can promise without hesitation,' said Razoumikhin sincerely. 'You know that you and your family are more important to me than anything in the world.'

'Yes, I know that,' thought Raskolnikoff, 'but what will you think, my friend, when you find out that I'm guilty of murder?'

The two friends arrived at the lodgings of Raskolnikoff's mother and sister at eight o'clock, at the exact moment that Peter Petrovitch Looshin arrived. Looshin, who was always concerned about doing things properly, was unsure of himself because he had warned Dounia that he would not stay in the same room with Raskolnikoff. Despite this, he began politely by asking Pulcheria Alexandrovna about their journey to St Petersburg.

'Our trip wasn't so bad, but after our arrival in this city our situation would have been terrible without the assistance of this kind young man, Dmitri Prokovitch Razoumikhin,' reported Pulcheria Alexandrovna.

Looshin was surprised by this bold statement, which he

interpreted as an insult to him, and silence filled the room. Finally, Raskolnikoff's mother realized that she would have to continue the conversation. 'Did you know that Marfa Petrovna is dead?' she asked Looshin.

'Yes, I did, and I've heard from reliable sources that her husband, Svidrigaïloff, is already here, in St Petersburg. I've even heard that there are suspicions that his actions may in some way have led to his wife's death. You must, Dounia, refuse to see him under any circumstances,' insisted Looshin. 'He's an evil man, possibly involved in the deaths of several other people.'

'Please, Peter Petrovitch, don't talk about that man,' cried Dounia. 'The subject is upsetting to me.'

Raskolnikoff surprised everyone by saying, 'He visited me today, asking for a meeting with Dounia. He has an offer for you, dear sister, which I'll explain later when we're alone, and he's told me that Marfa Petrovna left you 3,000 roubles, which you may collect immediately.'

These words obviously offended Looshin, and he looked at his watch. 'I have urgent business to attend to, so I won't disturb your private conversations any longer. Besides, I'd hoped to meet with you, Dounia, and your mother without your brother here. I'm very upset that you didn't agree to my request.'

'I admit that I asked Rodion to be here,' began Dounia, 'because I don't want any misunderstanding to exist between the two of you.'

'I'm sorry, Dounia,' explained Looshin, 'but your brother insulted me, and I can't forgive or forget such an offence.'

'Explain yourself,' said Dounia, 'and if an agreement can't be reached, I'll choose between you.'

'Love for your husband, the future companion of your life, must always be higher than love for your brother. He thinks my motives for marrying you are wicked, and this idea must have been given to him by your mother,' Looshin said.

'Peter Petrovitch,' interrupted Pulcheria Alexandrovna, 'I think our presence in St Petersburg is evidence that we trust you, but why have you accused my son of something that's false?'

'I'm sure I haven't lied about your son,' Looshin said.

'In your letter you told my mother that I gave twenty roubles to a young prostitute,' Raskolnikoff said, 'when you know I gave the money to help a widow and her children after their husband and father had been crushed under a carriage.'

'Do you deny throwing away your mother's money? Do you guarantee that every person in that family is respectable? Would you introduce that young prostitute to your mother and sister?' demanded Looshin.

'I've already done so. She sat down with them yesterday.'

Peter Petrovitch Looshin took his hat and walked towards the door. 'Dounia, I cannot be friends with your brother, and I'll leave so that you can discuss Svidrigaïloff's secret offer.'

'Peter Petrovitch, I'm ashamed to have been connected with you. Please leave this room!' Dounia said, looking pale with anger.

'Dounia Romanovna,' Looshin began, unable to believe that he was being rejected, 'if I go now, I'll never return. I mean what I say! And, you should remember that I asked you to marry me at a time when public opinion was against you. I expected you to be grateful, but now I see I was wrong to ignore public opinion.'

'I think you're asking for a fight!' shouted Raskolnikoff, approaching Looshin and speaking in his face. 'Leave now or I'll throw you down the stairs.'

Looshin, trembling with anger, turned and left, but his heart was full of hatred for Raskolnikoff, who he believed was completely responsible for his embarrassment.

Everyone in the little group was greatly relieved to see Looshin leave, but Raskolnikoff remained quiet and looked very serious. Dounia sat beside him and said, 'Dear brother, tell me what Svidrigaïloff said to you.'

'He insists that he will give you 10,000 roubles, and he's very anxious to meet with you.'

'She'll never see him!' cried Pulcheria Alexandrovna. 'How dare he offer her money!'

After hearing the whole story of her brother's meeting with Svidrigaïloff, Dounia said, 'I don't trust him. I'm afraid he has a secret plan.'

'Please don't worry, Dounia Romanovna,' said Razoumikhin, 'Rodion has asked me to protect you from this man, and I will with all my strength, now and always.'

Dounia held out her hand to Razoumikhin, and the two exchanged understanding smiles.

'I hope you'll stay in St Petersburg,' continued Razoumikhin. 'If we think about it hard enough, I'm sure we can find a way to make a living for all of us, perhaps by starting a small business for translating and publishing books. I expect to receive 1,000 roubles from an uncle very soon, and if you also choose to invest 1,000 roubles, that will be enough to get us started. We can be partners.'

'This sounds like a very good idea,' said Dounia. 'What do you think, Rodion?'

'I'm confident that Razoumikhin will lead you in the right direction.' Raskolnikoff got up and prepared to leave.

'Rodion, what's the matter? Where are you going now?' asked Dounia.

'It would be better if we separated for some time – I don't feel well, and I need to rest. I won't forget you, and I'll always love you, but please leave me alone now. Perhaps everything will be all right, and then I'll come back to you, but for now, if you love me, give up the idea of seeing me.'

'Rodion, please don't do this to our mother,' protested Dounia, but her brother walked out and closed the door behind him. 'He has no pity – he's selfish and has a hard heart.'

'No, Dounia, I'm afraid he's mad,' said Razoumikhin, as he hurried out of the door to find his friend.

Raskolnikoff was waiting for him on the street. 'I knew you'd come after me – you're a true friend. But please, listen. Don't question me, and please stay away from me – but can I ask you to promise again that you'll protect and care for my mother and sister?'

Standing in the dark street, the two friends looked at each other in silence, but Razoumikhin felt the force of Raskolnikoff's fierce look, which seemed to touch his soul. Suddenly he trembled and grew as pale as the moon; the terrible truth had been revealed to him.

'Do you understand me now?' Raskolnikoff asked.

Razoumikhin returned to the two ladies, becoming to them from that moment a son and a brother.

Raskolnikoff went straight to the river and found the house where Sonia was living.

'Who's there?' the girl asked when she heard his knock.

'It's me, Raskolnikoff. I need to talk to you.'

Sonia let him in, but stood frozen with fear. Even Raskolnikoff, who was accustomed to poverty, was shocked by the poor conditions in which Sonia lived. Her room reminded him of a peasant's hut, with very little furniture and filthy, dark walls marked by the damp air and coal smoke.

'Will you please sit down and allow me to talk to you?' Raskolnikoff asked gently. 'Do you have a good relationship with Catherine Ivanovna, Sonia? Do you like her?'

'Of course I do, I love her. She's like a little child because she believes in justice and thinks life will be good again one day.'

'But what's going to happen to Catherine Ivanovna and her children now? Can you feed them and pay their rent? I suppose she depends on you for everything.'

'Any money I have, I freely give her, but she's very ill and very sad. She coughs blood and today she fainted while cleaning the room in preparation for the meal that will follow my father's funeral.'

'She'll die before long,' Raskolnikoff said. 'Perhaps it would be better for all of you if she died soon, but what would you do with the children? You couldn't bring them here.'

'Don't talk like that. It can't happen – not yet. God will protect Catherine Ivanovna and the children,' said Sonia.

'Perhaps there is no God,' Raskolnikoff replied bitterly.

Sonia put her face in her hands and cried, but she remained silent. Raskolnikoff approached the girl and looked at her face, bathed in tears. Then he knelt in front of her, leaned over and kissed her feet. Looking frightened, Sonia moved away, as if to escape from a madman. 'What are you doing?' she cried.

'I didn't bow down to you personally, but to the suffering humanity that you represent. I thought only of your pain, caused by your sacrifice for others. I can see into your heart: your sin hasn't touched your good, sweet soul.' Then he asked, 'Sonia, do you often pray to God?'

'What would I be without God?' whispered the girl, while looking at Raskolnikoff and reaching out to grip his hand. 'God does everything for me.'

'Mad! She must be mad,' Raskolnikoff thought, withdrawing his hand and walking round Sonia's tiny room. He stopped and picked up her Bible, asking, 'Where did you get this from?'

'My friend Elizabeth lent it to me before she was killed with a hatchet.'

'How strange! I'm the cause of so much suffering,' thought Raskolnikoff, as he pictured the hatchet falling on Elizabeth's innocent skull. He felt weak.

He held the book in front of Sonia and ordered, 'Find the story of Lazarus, the man who Jesus brought back to life after four days in the grave – find it and read it to me.'

In a trembling voice, Sonia read the dramatic story of the death and resurrection of Lazarus, but she gained confidence when she read the words of Jesus: 'I am the resurrection, and the life; whoever believes in me, though he were dead, shall live; and whoever lives and believes in me shall never die.' Sonia's voice was strong and full of joy, as if these words were her own declaration of faith. After closing the book, she sat quietly as the excitement she felt from having read the story died down.

Suddenly Raskolnikoff rose and said in a loud voice, 'I came to speak to you about an urgent matter. This evening I've broken all ties with my mother and sister – I shan't speak to them or see them again. From today, you're all that's left to me. Don't you see, we're both cursed, so let's begin again – let's go away together.'

Raskolnikoff's words frightened Sonia. She could see that he was extremely unhappy, and she thought he must also be mad, but she asked, 'What are you talking about? Where would we go?'

'I don't know, but I know that the way and the goal are the same for us. We understand and need each other. You've destroyed a life – your own – and if you continue living as you do, you'll go mad. Stop relying on God and look at your life in a true light and escape from here with me.'

'What would happen to Catherine Ivanovna and the children?'

'Cut all ties to your family and move forward. Our goal is freedom and power, but especially power, to control our little world. I must go now and I might not return, but if I do, you'll find out who killed your friend Elizabeth.'

Sonia looked at him in terror. 'Do you really know who murdered her?'

'Yes, and I shall reveal it to you alone! I selected you the first time I heard your father speak about you – but for now, goodbye.'

Sonia was left with many things to consider: Did he really know who had killed Elizabeth? Why had he separated himself from his family? Why had he kissed her feet and talked of going somewhere together? Was he completely mad?

But Sonia was not the only person with these questions on their mind. During Raskolnikoff's visit, her next-door neighbour, Svidrigaïloff, had been on the other side of her thin wall, listening to every word Raskolnikoff and Sonia said. Now he planned to be at home the next day in case Raskolnikoff returned with even more interesting information.

♦

The next morning Raskolnikoff went to Porphyrius Petrovitch's office, determined to find out if the stranger who had accused him of being a murderer had been to see the magistrate with the same information. After quite a long wait, during which Raskolnikoff had time to become fearful again, Porphyrius Petrovitch called the young man into his office, welcoming him as if he were a close friend. 'Hello, my dear Raskolnikoff, how good to see you again. Please, sit here on the sofa.'

This friendly attitude made Raskolnikoff nervous, but he sat down and said, 'I've brought the letter about my pawned items. I hope it's satisfactory.'

'Oh, yes, yes, I'm sure it's fine,' answered the magistrate, locking the paper in his desk drawer, and then walking round the room instead of sitting down.

'Yesterday,' Raskolnikoff began nervously, 'you mentioned a wish to question me about my business with the murder victim, Alena Ivanovna.'

'No hurry about that, I assure you. Would you like a cigarette? No, you don't smoke, do you? What do you think of my office? Very grand for a government office, don't you think?'

'Are you playing with me again?' asked Raskolnikoff boldly.

'Do all magistrates chat and gossip about nothing before crushing the accused with a serious question?'

Porphyrius Petrovitch looked at his visitor and burst out laughing, but Raskolnikoff was very serious and said, 'Porphyrius Petrovitch, I have a funeral to go to, so please either question me directly and immediately, or let me go.'

'Question you about what?' the magistrate asked. 'The matter is of very little importance, so relax and don't be so easily offended. You were studying law, weren't you, and I enjoyed your interpretation of my questions, so please stay a little longer and chat with me as a friend.' Having said that, Porphyrius Petrovitch continued to talk about the practice of law as he walked around his office, stopping from time to time near one of the two doors and seeming to listen.

'Is he expecting something to happen?' Raskolnikoff wondered.

'Of course I can't teach you anything about the law, since your articles get published in law journals,' Porphyrius Petrovitch was saying, 'but imagine a case in which I, as a magistrate, was sure that a man was guilty of a certain crime, even without having definite proof. I would take my time in questioning this man because first, I wouldn't want to make him defensive, and second, I would want to have definite proof before I arrested him. If he knew I was watching him, although I hadn't accused him, he would eventually lose his self-control and show me the necessary evidence. It doesn't matter if the suspect is a poor man who can neither read nor write or a famous intellectual. He's my victim, from a psychological point of view, and he knows it. He wouldn't escape even if he could, but instead he would come closer and closer to me, and finally – bang! – he would prove his own guilt.'

Raskolnikoff knew he was being played with again, and he made himself stay calm and quiet, feeling sure that Porphyrius Petrovitch was trying to do more than frighten him. Finally, though, he stood up and shouted, 'I believe you suspect me of having murdered the old moneylender and her sister. I've had enough of your games – I won't permit you to torture me this way.'

'Rodion Romanovitch! My dear friend! Please calm down. If you go on like this, you'll go mad. You're as excited as Dmitri Prokovitch Razoumikhin was when he came to see me.'

'And what did you learn from him?'

'I know that you went to Alena Ivanovna's building at ten o'clock two nights ago, asking about renting her empty rooms and about what had happened to the blood left on the floor after her murder. Your actions have upset your good friend because you've made him suspect you, but I know that your actions have been caused by your illness.'

'I wasn't ill two nights ago. I was perfectly sane and knew what I was doing. Do you hear me?' demanded Raskolnikoff.

'Rodion Romanovitch, you must understand that I take a sincere interest in you and wish you well, so take my advice and see a doctor. And another thing – hasn't your family moved to St Petersburg? You should be the cause of their happiness, not their anxiety.'

'Why is that any of your business? Have you been watching me? Am I your suspect?'

'My dear fellow, you're very intelligent but have a lot to learn about how we deal with murder cases. If you were a suspect, I would have dealt with you quite differently and would have collected enough evidence to have arrested you by now. But you're ill – you need rest before you'll be able to interpret things logically.'

'Stop lying to me,' Raskolnikoff said. 'Please answer one question truthfully: Am I a suspect in this murder case?'

'Why do you wish to know so much? Haven't we left you in peace? You've come here twice, both times without being summoned. Please, tell me your reasons.'

'I can no longer bear . . .'

'Uncertainty?' interrupted the magistrate.

'I won't permit you to torture me in this way. Arrest me, search me, but stop playing games with me, and understand that I'm not your friend,' Raskolnikoff said, as he stood up and moved towards the door.

'Wait,' Porphyrius Petrovitch said with a smile, 'I have a surprise for you behind that door.'

'You're lying again. You keep lying, hoping that I'll say something to connect me to those murders, but you have no evidence, no witnesses.'

Both men stopped talking and listened when they heard a noise behind the second door.

'Who's there? What's your surprise? If you have a witness, let him in. I'm ready,' said Raskolnikoff.

But instead of Porphyrius Petrovitch's planned surprise, the second door flew open and a man burst into the room, followed by a police officer, who was trying to grab him.

'What's the meaning of this?' asked the magistrate, greatly annoyed. 'You're early. Take this prisoner away and keep him out of my sight until I call for him.'

But the prisoner fell on his knees and shouted, 'I'm guilty. I'm the murderer.'

'What? Who have you murdered?' asked Porphyrius Petrovitch, clearly astonished.

'I killed Alena Ivanovna and her sister. I crushed their skulls with a hatchet while I was mad,' the prisoner stated clearly.

'Who are you? What's your name?'

'My name is Nikola,' the strange young man said. 'I'm a painter and was working with my friend Dmitri in the building where I murdered the women. But Dmitri is innocent. He knew nothing about my crime.'

'That's enough!' shouted Porphyrius Petrovitch angrily. 'The man isn't telling the truth.' Then he looked at Raskolnikoff, whom he had forgotten about temporarily. 'Rodion Romanovitch, please excuse me. Come back another day, and we'll chat again. I may even have a few more questions for you.'

'I see we're likely to become close friends with all these meetings,' Raskolnikoff joked, now that he was escaping from the magistrate and his questions. 'Anyway, good luck with your prisoner. You must have worked hard on him to get him to confess, but now it's surprising to hear you doubt his story. Is this another of your psychological tricks?'

'I'm glad you see a funny side to my investigations,' the magistrate said as Raskolnikoff left.

Neither man had found their meeting satisfactory, and Raskolnikoff analysed what had been said as he walked towards his lodgings. At least he would not be arrested today and charged with murder, though he did not feel secure about the next day. But even this temporary peace was disturbed when he found the man who had called him murderer waiting outside his room.

'What do you want?' asked Raskolnikoff, his heart pounding violently.

The man bowed and said, 'I ask you to pardon me for accusing you. I saw you two nights ago at the building where Alena Ivanovna lived, but that was the only time I'd seen you.'

'Did you tell the magistrate, Porphyrius Petrovitch, that you saw me at that building two nights ago?'

'Yes, I told him today, just before you arrived at his office. I heard your conversation because he made me hide behind a door when you came in. After you left, he dismissed me too.'

'So you were the surprise, but you don't actually have any evidence to link me to the murders.'

'That's true, so I ask you to forgive me for any wrong I might have done to you.'

'May God forgive you,' replied Raskolnikoff, and with new hope he went back out into the street with his visitor.

Chapter 5 Confession

After separating from his former accuser, Raskolnikoff hurried to Catherine Ivanovna's lodgings to pay his respects to his friend Marmeladoff, who had just been buried. He was amazed to see the extraordinary meal and the great variety of drink that the widow had paid for with his money. Perhaps out of pride she felt that this – and inviting all her neighbours – was the only decent way to behave in these circumstances.

Catherine Ivanovna was delighted to see Raskolnikoff, in her opinion an educated man of culture. She was disappointed in the quality of most of the other guests – they seemed to have come only for the free food and drink – and Raskolnikoff spoke to her in a sincere and sympathetic manner, which most of the other guests had not even attempted. She seated him on her left and tried to make polite conversation with him, but her coughing, which had grown noticeably worse over the last two days, constantly interrupted her and often prevented her from finishing a sentence.

When she paused to catch her breath, Raskolnikoff asked where Sonia was.

'Look!' Catherine Ivanovna managed to say between coughs. 'Here she is now. Please, Sonia, sit down next to Rodion Romanovitch, a true friend to your dear father. Mr Raskolnikoff, do you know what my plans are for our future? I'm going to take my children and Sonia and return to the village where I grew up,' the young widow said, looking into the distance, as if picturing this impossible dream. 'I have friends there – people who knew my father – and with their help Sonia and I will open a school for young ladies. Sonia is so gentle and patient, and very intelligent – she'll manage the whole business for me.' Having said that, Catherine Ivanovna kissed Sonia's cheek and burst into tears.

'I'm sorry, but my nerves are greatly excited, and I'm so tired that I can do no more. Can we get rid of these guests?' Catherine Ivanovna asked. She lay down on her bed in the corner and soon found herself alone with her hopes for the future and her three small children.

Quickly, though temporarily, forgetting about the widow and her troubles, Raskolnikoff left the building and hurried towards Sonia's lodgings. Catherine Ivanovna, with her poor health and her unreal hopes, had greatly disturbed the girl, and she had left before Raskolnikoff, needing some time alone to think about her father and about her own future, which she knew would be on the streets of St Petersburg and not in a school for young ladies. What she did not know was that Raskolnikoff was coming to visit her again, and that this time he would leave her with an even greater burden because he was determined to confess everything to her.

When Raskolnikoff arrived at Sonia's room, she greeted him warmly and thanked him for attending Catherine Ivanovna's dinner and for treating both her stepmother and herself with respect and kindness.

'Sonia, I'd like to know how you'd solve a certain problem: Suppose Catherine Ivanovna and the children were thrown out of their lodgings by an evil landlord who left them starving on the street. And imagine that, as a consequence, Catherine's oldest child, Polenka, had to work on the streets, like you. And, suppose that you could save your stepmother and the children by killing the man who'd caused their ruin. I'm anxious to know what action you'd take.'

'Why are you asking me to make a decision about a person who doesn't exist, about a problem that may never exist? Anyway, why should I have to decide if a person should live or die? Have you only come here to torture me?' Sonia asked, as she burst into tears.

Raskolnikoff watched her cry and found himself thinking that he was beginning to hate the girl, but when she looked directly at him, he saw a look of anxious love in her eyes. The hatred quickly faded from his heart, and once again he decided that he must confess his crimes to Sonia.

'What's the matter?' she asked, puzzled and disturbed by his changing moods.

'Nothing, Sonia, please don't be afraid,' he said, but he now sounded frightened himself.

'Oh, Rodion Romanovitch, you suffer so much.'

'It's nothing! But do you remember I told you that if I came here today, I'd tell you who killed your friend Elizabeth? That's why I'm here now.'

'How do you know who the murderer is?' Sonia asked, growing paler and more nervous. 'Has he been arrested?'

'No, he hasn't, but I know who it is,' Raskolnikoff said, looking at her with a strange smile on his lips. 'It's someone I know very well, someone who hadn't planned to murder her, someone who had only planned to murder the old woman when she was at home alone. He only killed Elizabeth because she surprised him – he was there when she came home and he killed her. Guess who it was!' He continued to stare at her and suddenly read on her face a look of terrible fear, just like the look he had seen on Elizabeth's face when he had raised the hatchet above her skull to kill her. 'Sonia, have you guessed?'

'My God!' Sonia whispered and fell back on to her bed, but she rose almost immediately and went to him, seizing his hands and looking deeply into his eyes. Had she made a mistake? She hoped so, but when she looked at Raskolnikoff's face, her suspicion became certainty. She fell on her knees in front of him. 'You are lost!' she cried. But then she put her arms around his neck and kissed him gently, like a mother kissing her baby. 'At this moment, you must be the most miserable man on earth,' she said, as she held him in her arms.

Raskolnikoff felt his heart grow warm under the influence of an emotion that he had not felt for a long time. He struggled to speak as tears fell from his eyes. 'Sonia, will you stay with me? You won't abandon me, will you?'

'No, never!' she cried. 'I'll follow you wherever you go, even to Siberia* or to your death.'

The mention of death caused Raskolnikoff a painful feeling, and a bitter, almost proud, smile appeared on his lips. 'Perhaps I'm not ready for death, Sonia,' he said.

She had thought only of his pain and suffering. This statement, and his tone of voice, reminded her that he was a murderer. 'How is it possible that you could kill two people? Were you hungry? Did you want to find money to help your mother? Ah!' she cried suddenly. 'Was the money you gave Catherine Ivanovna from the old woman's flat?'

'No, Sonia, that money came from my mother. The money and jewellery I took from Alena Ivanovna is hidden. I haven't spent any of it, even though I went to her flat to steal, as well as to kill – but the stealing wasn't important to me. If it had been, I'd be happy now, but you can see that I'm miserable. If my only motive in committing murder had been to obtain money, I would be happy now. But I suffer more each day, and because of that I came to you yesterday and asked you to go away with me. I need your promise that you'll never leave me.' Sonia took his hand as he continued in a desperate voice, 'Please don't cry, Sonia. I know I'm asking too much of you. My courage has failed, so I've asked you to share my burden. Can you help me? Can you love a coward like me?'

* Siberia: a cold, isolated region of central and eastern Russia, used in the past as a place of punishment to send criminals to

'Explain everything to me, please,' Sonia said. 'I want to understand.'

'I wanted to be an extraordinary man, someone who could change the world. Can you understand that?'

'No, I can't,' Sonia admitted, 'but continue, and I'll understand everything.'

'You're right – that was ridiculous. I wanted to help my mother and sister – I wanted to save my sister from sacrificing herself for my sake. I wanted to protect my own future and go back to university, get a job one day, marry and have children. I thought the old witch's money would get me started in life, that was all, but I admit it was wrong to kill her.' Raskolnikoff lowered his head, exhausted.

'No, that's still not a good enough reason – tell me the whole truth,' insisted Sonia.

'Sonia, I only killed a miserable creature, a louse that no one would miss, but you're right, that's not the whole reason either. Perhaps I'm very proud, and full of envy, and foolish. When I was forced to leave university, I went to my room and stayed there. I stopped eating, stopped going out, stopped seeing anyone, and then I started thinking and came to the conclusion that the man who dares much is a man who will gain respect and power.

'I longed to have enough courage to seize power, to dare to do something extraordinary, so I committed murder. That was my only motive: to do something extraordinary, something I did for myself and for no other reason. It was an experiment to find out if I was a man – or a louse, like everyone else.'

'But you had no right to kill!' cried Sonia, amazed at Raskolnikoff's excuses.

'But wait, did I really kill the old woman? No, I killed myself – I'm the one who's been totally ruined and driven mad. Now I've said enough, Sonia – please leave me alone!' Raskolnikoff said, as he hid his face in his hands and cried softly.

'How he's suffering!' thought Sonia.

'Sonia, tell me what I should do now, please,' Raskolnikoff said, as he suddenly raised his head.

Sonia's face lit up and she seized Raskolnikoff by the shoulders and said, 'Rise!' He was astonished by her now, but did as she instructed. 'Go immediately to the nearest public square and fall to your knees. Kiss the earth, which you have stained, and shout to everyone, "I am a murderer!" and God will give you peace again. Will you go?' she asked, staring at him with fire in her eyes.

'Do you want me to be hanged?' Raskolnikoff asked, astonished.

'I want you to seek redemption, to be saved!'

'Sonia, I won't accuse myself.'

'But how can you live? You've already left your mother and sister because you couldn't face them. What will become of a man whose sin stops him from living in this world?'

'I won't give myself up to the police. What should I say to them? That I'm guilty of murder and, not daring to benefit from the stolen money, hid it under a stone? They'd think I was a fool.'

'But you can't live with your burden for a lifetime.'

'I'll get used to it, but anyway, I think I'll be arrested soon – maybe even today. The police are looking for me. Don't worry, they won't be able to keep me in prison because they don't have any evidence against me, but will you visit me while I'm there?'

'Yes! Yes!'

But at that moment Raskolnikoff changed his mind. She had given him her whole heart, and he realized that he was more unhappy than ever. 'Sonia, it would be better if you didn't visit me in prison.'

They sat, quiet and sad, beside each other, and then Sonia said, 'Please take this wooden cross and wear it.'

'Not now, Sonia. I'll take it when I'm ready to confess.'

At that moment they were interrupted by three knocks on the door.

'Sonia Semenovna, come quickly! Your stepmother has gone completely mad,' reported a young man, one of Catherine Ivanovna's neighbours.

The girl screamed and seized the neighbour's arm. 'What's happened? Where is she?'

'After all the guests left, the landlady demanded the rent from Catherine Ivanovna, and when she said she didn't have any more money, that cruel woman threw Mrs Marmeladoff and the children into the street. She's now dragging those poor children round the city, making them sing and dance and beg in the street!'

Sonia grabbed her coat and hurried out of the house with Raskolnikoff and the other young man following her, but instead of accompanying Sonia in her search for the widow and her children, Raskolnikoff returned to his own room and thought about his meeting with Sonia. He had burdened her with his unhappiness and now, again, felt hatred for her. He decided to isolate himself from her as well as from the rest of the world.

Suddenly the door opened and his sister walked in. She sat down opposite Raskolnikoff. 'Don't be upset with me, dear brother,' Dounia began in an affectionate voice, 'but I want you to know that Razoumikhin has told me that you've been questioned and that the police suspect you of being involved in those murders, but Dmitri Prokovitch and I believe in you – we know that you're innocent. Now I understand why you've separated yourself from us, but I must ask you for two favours. First, our mother knows nothing about this terrible situation, and I'll protect her from it, but please visit her at least one more time. Second, I beg you to remember that if you need me, I'll come to you and help you in any way possible. Goodbye!' She turned and quickly moved towards the door.

'Dounia!' Raskolnikoff called to her. 'Dmitri Prokovitch Razoumikhin is an excellent man: ambitious, hard-working, honest and sincere. Remember that.'

The girl blushed but then said, in a voice trembling with fear, 'I hope this doesn't mean we're parting forever.'

'Goodbye,' Raskolnikoff said simply.

After Dounia left, Raskolnikoff stayed in his room alone until his thoughts about confession and redemption drove him outside once more. Almost immediately, he met Catherine Ivanovna's neighbour, who was looking for him.

'Please, can you come and help us? We've found Catherine Ivanovna and the children, and if we don't get them off the street, the police will surely arrest them.'

The two young men found Sonia with the little family on a busy street near the bridge over the River Neva. The young widow was exhausted and very ill, but she constantly shouted at her children and beat them if they stopped their singing and dancing. Sonia remained at her side, trying to persuade her to come to her lodgings and rest.

'Don't talk to me, Sonia!' Catherine Ivanovna said between shouting and coughing. 'It's better for the public to see us and to feel embarrassed that this has happened to people from a cultured background. But look at them, they're laughing at us, and nobody will help us – we've only collected two kopecks! Cruel, uncivilized, unfeeling animals! We must move on to a better neighbourhood where people will recognize that we deserve their charity. Perhaps the children could sing a French song to impress them.'

Catherine Ivanovna was interrupted by a police officer, who said, 'It's against the law to disturb the peace. Please behave yourself and take these children home.'

'Home? I have no home. I buried my husband today, and now I must feed my children,' Catherine Ivanovna responded.

'I'm sorry, madam, but you're causing a crowd to gather, and you're a public nuisance. I can see that you're ill, so allow me to help you to your house.'

Another policeman approached the growing crowd, frightening the children, who ran off. Catherine Ivanovna tried to run after them but tripped and fell, and Sonia, reaching her, saw that her dress was covered in blood. Raskolnikoff and the neighbour arrived at this moment and helped Sonia get Catherine and the children to Sonia's lodgings. As they laid the young widow on the sofa, the neighbour said, 'She didn't cut herself when she fell; the blood is coming from her lungs. I'm afraid she won't live much longer.'

After a few minutes, the flow of blood stopped and Catherine Ivanovna was able to speak in a whisper. 'Are my children here? Dear Sonia, I leave these orphans in your hands. I'm finished. Let me die in peace,' and saying that, Catherine Ivanovna fell back on the pillow and died.

Sonia, more dead than alive herself, held her stepmother's body tenderly, while the children, troubled by all that had happened in a very eventful day, cried and kissed their dead mother.

Several of Sonia's neighbours had crowded round the door of her room to find out what the excitement was about. Noticeable in this crowd was the healthy, well-dressed figure of Svidrigaïloff, who now approached Raskolnikoff. 'Rodion Romanovitch, I want a private word with you. I'll take responsibility for this whole business – I mean the funeral and everything. I'll put the three children in a good home for orphans and will invest money for Sonia so she'll be able to live a decent life on the interest it will earn.'

'Why are you being so generous?'

'As I told you, I have plenty of money, and since your sister won't accept the 10,000 roubles I offered her, I'll use it for this purpose. Admit that I can act unselfishly – perhaps do something extraordinary.'

Raskolnikoff's heart pounded in his chest and he felt cold. 'Why do you say that? What are you talking about?'

'I'm talking about helping the children and Sonia. She's a good creature, not a louse like a certain old moneylender. By the way, did you know that I'm living at present in the rooms next to Sonia's, and this building has very thin walls. I told you that you interest me, and today my interest in you has greatly increased.'

Chapter 6   Fate

During the next two days Raskolnikoff avoided contact with people more than ever, but this did not stop him from worrying about what Svidrigaïloff had said to him after the death of Catherine Ivanovna. His concerns increased because he accidentally met Svidrigaïloff twice before the young widow was buried. On the second occasion, as they were both entering the building where Sonia lived, the older man asked, 'Rodion Romanovitch, what's happened to you? You seem to be walking around in a fog. You need to wake up and live life to the fullest. And remember,' he said mysteriously, 'it's necessary for a man to have air – air alone, all air.'

Trying to interpret this strange advice, Raskolnikoff remained alone, walking among the crowds on the busy city streets or sitting silently in cheap taverns. On the morning of Catherine Ivanovna's funeral, he woke up towards dawn under a tree near the river and felt that his fever had returned. He struggled to get back to his room, where he slept on his little sofa until two o'clock in the afternoon. Nastasia brought him his dinner and, unexpectedly, he was eating with a better appetite than he had had for many days, when Razoumikhin came through his door.

'Oh, so you're finally at home, and eating, are you? I suppose you're not ill then,' Razoumikhin said in a serious voice. 'I've come for only one reason: to find out whether or not you're completely out of your mind, because I can't believe anyone would treat your mother and sister as badly as you've done unless he were mad. Your mother was very worried about you and came here with me last evening to see if you were still alive, but your room was empty and your mother reached the conclusion that you simply didn't want to see her. Don't you have a conscience?'

'I spoke to my sister about you recently,' Raskolnikoff began. 'She came here alone, and we talked.'

'What did you say about me?' Razoumikhin asked.

'I told her that you're an excellent man, ambitious, hard-working, honest and sincere. I didn't tell her that you love her because she knows that, and I think she loves you too, so I'll repeat what I said once before: whatever happens to me, please take care of them. And don't worry about my secrets – everything will be worked out eventually. Yesterday a man told me that air was necessary to every man. I'm going to find him and ask him to explain what he meant.'

'Perhaps Dounia's letter came from a similar sort of man,' Razoumikhin said, almost to himself.

'What letter?' Raskolnikoff asked.

'A letter she received yesterday which upset her a lot, but which she hasn't discussed with me or your mother. And now I must return to them, but one more thing: Do you remember the murder case that Porphyrius Petrovitch was working on? Well, they've discovered who murdered the old woman and her sister,' Razoumikhin said, giving Raskolnikoff a knowing look. 'A man named Nikola, one of the two painters, has confessed to both murders.'

'How did you find out about this?' Raskolnikoff asked.

'Porphyrius himself told me when I was there with a small

group of friends. He explained the case very thoroughly, in psychological terms – you know his style. And now I'll say goodbye.'

After Razoumikhin had left, Raskolnikoff tried to decide how Porphyrius Petrovitch could believe for one moment in Nikola's guilt, but his thoughts were interrupted by the arrival of the magistrate himself at his door.

Porphyrius Petrovitch came in and sat down without being invited, and began talking immediately. 'I've called, my dear fellow because I owe you an explanation, even an apology, after our last meeting ended in such an unfriendly manner. No more scenes, no more clever games – instead, I hope we can be more open with each other.'

'What's your purpose in coming here?' asked Raskolnikoff.

'To explain things to you clearly and openly,' Porphyrius Petrovitch began again. 'I suspected you of the murder of Alena Ivanovna and her sister because of your behaviour at the police station and because later you visited the scene of the crime. Obviously, I had no clear evidence, but your article in the law journal, clearly written by someone who could one day make a real contribution to our country's legal system, seemed to have a possible connection to the motives behind the murders. After that I had this room searched and, as you can guess, we found nothing. But then the man who had accused you on the street came to me and told me that you were the murderer and described how you'd reacted to his accusation. Then I said to myself, "Raskolnikoff will visit me soon, without being asked. Other kinds of men wouldn't do so, but this one will," and you did – that same morning – and you enjoyed dropping hints about your role in the crime.'

'But Razoumikhin told me just now of your conviction that Nikola is guilty,' Raskolnikoff said, but he could not go on because his breath failed him.

'Let's leave Razoumikhin out of this, shall we? I had to tell him something because he was always coming to me and asking questions. Nikola's like a confused child. He drinks too much and is easily influenced, both by friends and by "religious" men. He wants to suffer and find redemption, and that was his idea in coming to the police and confessing. But in the end, the facts will show that Nikola couldn't have committed the murders.

'I believe our murderer is a theorist, an intellectual who was bold enough to put his theory to the test, but one who hasn't been able to live with his crime. He hasn't spent any of the money he stole, and he had to return to the scene of the crime, to ring the bell, to look for the blood. He doesn't think of himself as a murderer because he can explain his motives, but his actions are those of a diseased man.'

Raskolnikoff's whole body trembled, but he managed to ask, 'Then who committed the murders?'

Porphyrius Petrovitch, looking surprised at this question, said, 'It's obvious that you did – you and you alone.'

Both were silent and, strangely, this silence lasted for about ten minutes. Then Raskolnikoff cried angrily, 'If I'm the murderer, why haven't you arrested me?'

'I'll have you arrested eventually, but as someone who's sincerely interested in you, I recommend that you go to the police and confess to the murders. It's the wisest action for you to take.'

'But you don't have any solid evidence to prove that I murdered those two women.'

'Yes, Rodion Romanovitch, I do have the necessary proof, something that I found out the other day. God has sent it to me. But I won't tell you about it yet. Take my advice and confess now. I'll explain to the judges that illness and poverty led you to murder and, as a result, you'll have a shorter punishment.'

Smiling, Raskolnikoff said, 'I don't want a shorter sentence.'

'I was afraid that you'd refuse to take my advice,' Porphyrius Petrovitch said, with a sad look in his eyes. 'Stop torturing yourself. Don't hate life! You could still have a brilliant future and contribute much to our society. You won't be in prison forever, and you haven't really lived yet. You've tested a theory and failed, but you aren't a hopeless criminal – what you require at present is air. I think a change of environment will benefit you, will give you time to think, to plan and even to suffer for what you've done. And, suffering is a good thing. Then, after a time in prison, I believe you'll come out of this terrible darkness and love life again.'

'When do you propose arresting me?' asked Raskolnikoff.

'I can give you one or two days' freedom, but believe me, the advice I'm giving you is the very best for you to follow!'

'Before we part,' Raskolnikoff began, 'I want you to remember one thing: I haven't made a confession today.'

'I'll remember your words accurately, but may I ask one more thing of you? If you're tempted by suicide, could you please leave a note and tell us where you've hidden the money and jewellery? It would make my job a lot easier. But for now, goodbye, and may God send you good thoughts!'

Raskolnikoff went back into the street as soon as Porphyrius Petrovitch had left; he felt a need, something he could neither explain nor control, to see Svidrigaïloff, who both attracted and disgusted him. He knew that this man had heard him confess to the murders to Sonia, and he wanted to find out if he had gone to Porphyrius Petrovitch with this information.

Raskolnikoff now knew that he was in a dangerous position with regard to the police, but he was not sure if this bothered him or not, and he did not understand why he thought Svidrigaïloff – an offensive, unpleasant, even evil man – could possibly give him any advice or help. He wondered if this mysterious man somehow held a key to his fate, but he also wondered if Svidrigaïloff's only purpose in St Petersburg was to contact Dounia. Would he find a way to use Raskolnikoff's secret to get what he wanted from her? Was the letter that Dounia had received that morning from him? Raskolnikoff did not know the answer to these questions, but he knew that if this man hurt his sister in any way, he would not hesitate to kill him.

With little effort, he found Svidrigaïloff in a small, private room of a tavern. 'Rodion Romanovitch, how good to see you,' Svidrigaïloff said in greeting. 'Are you taking care of yourself? I blame your poor health on St Petersburg, a place where everyone seems depressed and a bit mad – perhaps as a result of the unfavourable climate.'

'I'm not here to talk about the weather,' Raskolnikoff began. 'I'm here to speak plainly to you with reference to my sister. If you plan to use the secret you know about me to make Dounia go away with you or anything else of that sort, I'll kill you, and I think you know that I'm capable of doing this.'

'Rodion Romanovitch, you misjudge me. It's true that I'm interested in you – Dounia told me a lot about you – but I don't mean any harm to you or to your family. I thought you might have something *new* to tell me, but now I suspect that you want me to tell *you* something new.'

'What new thing do you expect from me? Why have you come to the city at all?' Raskolnikoff asked.

'I'm not really sure. I don't have a clear identity – I'm not a country gentleman or a writer or a photographer. It's hard for a man to realize that he's nothing in particular. I thought you might guide me in a new direction. Perhaps I only came here for the women.'

'Women? But you've only recently buried your wife!'

'Don't act so shocked. I've never tried to hide the kind of man I am. My wife knew that I had my little romantic relationships with the servants, and she accepted that as part of my nature.

But your sister, the governess, was different – so handsome and intelligent – and Dounia tried to change me, to make me a better husband and a good man. She lectured me, but I listened only so that I could be alone with her. It was heaven, but I spoiled it all by my impatience. I swore my undying love and offered her my entire fortune if she'd run away with me; I knew she needed money to take care of her mother and you.'

'I can see that your only reason for coming here was to pursue my sister,' Raskolnikoff boldly accused the older man.

'Nonsense!' shouted Svidrigaïloff. 'Anyway, your sister can't bear the sight of me, and didn't I tell you that I'm going to get married? My future wife's family is very happy with the idea. As you might have guessed, they need money rather desperately, so they were pleased when I asked their youngest child – she'll be sixteen next month – to marry me. I don't know about your taste in women, but I find this teenager very fresh and charming, very willing to please me. Isn't that delicious?'

'Is it possible that you can seriously think of marrying a child of sixteen?' Raskolnikoff asked. 'Would your young wife be happy to know that my sister received a letter from you today?'

'You're a funny fellow,' Svidrigaïloff said thoughtfully. 'You judge me for planning to marry a young girl and for making her whole family's life better, but you ignore your own actions.'

'You shouldn't listen to people's private conversations,' Raskolnikoff whispered.

'Tell me, Rodion Romanovitch, which is the greater crime – listening to private conversations or murdering old women? I know what the magistrate would say, so consider escaping to America as soon as possible, which I'll gladly pay for. Your only alternative, if you're guilty of a crime, is to shoot yourself,' Svidrigaïloff said. 'That's what you want to do, isn't it?'

'I'm not thinking of committing suicide,' Raskolnikoff said quietly, ending the conversation and leaving Svidrigaïloff.

The younger man walked slowly towards the bridge with his head down, thinking over all the things Svidrigaïloff had said. Meanwhile, the older man hurried to a corner where he had arranged to meet someone. Soon he saw the person he was waiting for coming towards him.

'I've just had a chat with your brother,' the man said. 'He seemed very suspicious of me – did you tell him that I'd written to you?'

'Of course not,' Dounia said, 'but please make this quick. Tell me what you know about Rodion.'

'It's a private matter that I'd prefer not to discuss in a public place. If you want to know your brother's secret and how you can help him, you must come with me to my lodgings. What are you afraid of? We're not in the country here, and even in the country you did me more harm than I did to you. Don't be scared – Sonia Semenovna will be next door, and the whole building is full of people. Is there really anything so terrible about me?'

Dounia hesitated and looked closely at Svidrigaïloff. She knew him well and did not want to be alone with him in his rooms, but she had to find out what he knew about her brother. 'I know you're a man without honour, but I'm not afraid of you,' insisted Dounia proudly.

Svidrigaïloff tried to smile, but his face refused to obey him, and his heart beat wildly as he hurried Dounia to his lodgings.

After entering Svidrigaïloff's rooms, the man and woman sat at a distance from each other, but even this did not reduce the tense atmosphere, both physical and emotional, that spread through the room. Dounia could not hear any noise from the neighbouring rooms, and the feeling of being in an isolated, dangerous situation began to frighten her, but she put her fears to one side.

'In your letter,' Dounia began, 'you hint that my brother has committed a serious crime. I've heard similar rumours already, and I must tell you that I don't believe them.'

'I'm surprised that you're here if you're so certain that he's innocent. Your brother came to visit Sonia Semenovna and told her everything. I heard it all too, because I was sitting on this side of that very thin wall. He murdered the old moneylender and her sister and stole money and jewellery from their flat. Sonia was as frightened as you are now, but she won't reveal his secret.'

Dounia stood up and went to the door. 'I must talk to Sonia.'

'She won't be in her room,' the man said. 'She's gone out of town to help settle Catherine Ivanovna's orphans in their new home. She won't be back for hours. We're completely alone.'

'You always lie to me. I don't believe anything you say! And why have you locked this door?' Dounia shouted.

'Be calm, Dounia Romanovna, the door's locked so that we can talk without being disturbed. Listen, I'll help your brother if he'll let me. And anyway, he can do good deeds to wipe out his crime, and one day he may still become a great man.'

'How can you save him?'

'That depends on you and you alone,' Svidrigaïloff insisted in a quiet voice. 'I have friends and money, and with these I can move him out of Russia to a safe place. I can get a passport for him, and even for you and your mother if you choose to go with him – but you must allow me to love you.' His eyes shone brightly and he found it difficult to continue speaking. 'You – one word from you, and he's saved! I love you truly and will love you always. Speak and I'll obey your commands, but don't look at me with hatred. You're killing me!'

'Open the door at once,' Dounia screamed, shaking it with all her strength. 'I must find Rodion.'

'I've lost the key.'

'Then this is a trap?' Dounia cried, rushing into a corner of the room and trying to protect herself behind a small table. She was afraid that Svidrigaïloff might be going mad.

'I suppose it *is* a trap, but think about what I'm offering you. You can save your brother and your mother, and I'll treat you like a queen for the rest of your life. Don't fight against me, Dounia Romanovna – we're completely alone, and I'm at least twice as strong as you. No one would believe that I attacked you – a woman who was willing to come to my rooms.'

Dounia looked back at Svidrigaïloff with hatred in her eyes. She knew his true character and would never accept any deal that he might offer her, or give in to his demands for love. Suddenly she took a small gun from her pocket and placed it on the table in front of her.

Svidrigaïloff gave a cry of surprise. 'My dear, I think your little surprise gives me my answer and, if I'm not mistaken, that's my gun,' he said.

'It's not yours, but Marfa Petrovna's, who you stole from and poisoned, you disgusting man. How can *you* accuse my brother of anything?'

'If I committed any crime, I must have done it for you. And why not? I watched you in the evenings when the moon was shining. Your eyes were full of emotion, even love.'

'You lie! I've always hated you!' screamed Dounia.

'All right, I've lied, so fire your gun, you handsome creature. What are you waiting for?' he asked.

Dounia picked up the gun and aimed it at Svidrigaïloff. She was blushing deeply, trembling with emotion, and looked more beautiful than ever to the man in front of her. When he took a step towards her, she fired the gun and the bullet lightly scratched the right side of his forehead. He wiped the blood away with his handkerchief and said, 'That was nothing. Fire again or I'll seize you before you can defend yourself.' He moved two steps closer.

'Get away from me!' Dounia cried desperately. 'I swear I'll kill you!' She fired again, but the gun failed to go off and she threw it on the table. Svidrigaïloff approached her and, putting his arm around her, was surprised that she did not resist his tender touch.

In a gentle voice, she finally begged, 'Let me go.'

'Could you ever love me?' Svidrigaïloff asked. His heart pounded wildly as he waited for her answer.

'No, never,' she answered softly.

Svidrigaïloff removed his arm from Dounia's waist, walked away and stood silently at the window for a moment before saying very quietly, 'Here's the key. Take it and go quickly.'

After Dounia had left, Svidrigaïloff picked up the gun and found that it still contained two bullets. He put the weapon in his coat pocket and left his lodgings.

Until ten o'clock that night, Svidrigaïloff went from tavern to tavern, buying drinks for people but never taking a single drop of wine for himself. When he returned to his lodgings, he found that Sonia was in her room and he knocked on her door.

'Sonia Semenovna, perhaps I'll be going to America very soon, and I want to settle a few things before I go. I assume that Catherine Ivanovna's children are now happy and safe in their new home?'

'Yes, sir, they're very well looked after now – thank you, sir.'

'Before I go, I also want to provide for you. You can't go on living as you're doing now. Take this money and ask Dmitri Prokovitch Razoumikhin to look after it for you. Then you can do what you like and go where you like. I know Rodion Romanovitch's whole story but – trust me – I shan't say anything about his crime. Of course, he should confess everything, as you recommended, and take his punishment. I know that if he goes to Siberia, you'll go with him, so please accept this money.'

'How can I ever thank you?'

'Remember me to Rodion Romanovitch,' Svidrigaïloff said, and left.

Although it was now very late for a social call, Svidrigaïloff went directly to the home of his future wife. Her parents said that she was already in bed, but he insisted on seeing her. He informed the girl, in the presence of her father and mother, that he had to leave St Petersburg for a time because of important business elsewhere, but before departing he presented his future bride with 15,000 roubles which, he explained, was part of his wedding gift to her. He kissed the girl and left, thinking with genuine disgust that his present would surely be kept under lock and key by the parents.

By midnight Svidrigaïloff was completely alone in a dark, miserable room in a cheap hotel near the river. He soon fell asleep, but was tortured by terrible dreams of his past sins. Finally he woke and sat at the small table beside the window, looking out at the thick fog over the river as dawn began to break. He stood up and put on his coat, checked that the gun was in his pocket, left some money on the table and went outside.

He walked along the river until he came to a building with a soldier standing guard outside. 'This place suits me,' he said to himself, 'and the thing can be officially reported by a reliable witness.' Smiling at the soldier, he said, 'Good morning.'

'What do you want?' the man asked, without moving.

'I'm going to America. If anyone asks you, tell them that's where I've gone,' Svidrigaïloff said, taking the gun from his pocket.

'None of that nonsense here, sir!' the soldier shouted.

'This place suits me very well,' Svidrigaïloff said, as he held the gun to his head and fired.

◆

Earlier the same day, Raskolnikoff finally moved from his lonely position on the bridge and went to the new lodgings that Razoumikhin had found for his mother and sister. With relief, he found that his mother was in the flat alone.

Pulcheria Alexandrovna was astonished to see her son, but soon recovered herself, seized his hand and pulled him into her sitting room. 'Here you are at last! I'm so happy to see you. I won't question you or be angry with you. I've even read your article in the law journal three times, and of course I don't understand it all, not being an intellectual like you, but I feel so proud of you and what you've achieved. I can't believe anyone would think that someone as intelligent as you could be mad, just because of the way you live and dress.'

'Where's Dounia, Mother?' Raskolnikoff asked.

'She's out, and she never tells me where she's going or what business she has to take care of, but I know that she's very clever and loves both you and me. That's all I ask from you, Rodion – not that you visit often, but that you let me know that you love me – and an occasional visit, please,' Pulcheria Alexandrovna said, bursting into tears. 'Oh, I'm sorry, my son, don't worry about my tears. I'm just so happy to see you.'

'Mother, I assure you that I love you and always will. I came today to ask you one question. Will you love me as much as you do now whatever happens?'

Pulcheria Alexandrovna held her son in her arms and kissed him tenderly. 'I'll never stop loving you, but I worry about you too. You're going away, aren't you, Rodion?'

'Yes, I am.'

'I thought so, but where are you going? Can Dounia and I come with you?'

'Goodbye, Mother, I must leave you now,' said the son.

'Please, let me come with you,' the mother begged.

'No, but would you pray to God for me? Perhaps he'll hear your prayer,' and saying this, Raskolnikoff fell to the floor and kissed his mother's feet before rising and departing.

Raskolnikoff hurried towards his lodgings, determined to finish everything that day. He felt upset when he opened the door to his room and found his sister waiting for him. The sadness in her face showed him that she knew it all.

'I waited several hours at Sonia Semenovna's room, but you didn't arrive. Where have you been?' asked Dounia.

'I hardly know where I've been. I thought about jumping off the bridge and settling things that way, but, as you see, here I am,' Raskolnikoff said.

'That's what Sonia and I were worried about,' said Dounia. 'Thank God you're all right. And have you now decided to seek redemption?'

'Without delay. A courageous man ought not to fear shame. Can you still hold my hand?' he asked his sister.

'Have you ever doubted it?' Dounia asked, pressing his hand to her heart. 'Your confession will wash away half your crime.'

'Is it a crime to kill a disgusting old moneylender who, like a louse, lived on the blood of her victims? I'm ready to confess that I killed her, but I won't call my act a crime.'

'Rodion, you're guilty of spilling blood!' objected Dounia.

'I suppose I am, but look at history before you judge me. Men who have spilt blood, who have taken lives, often become the rulers of a country because they benefited mankind. I wanted to do that too – I wanted to help society by ridding it of that terrible witch, and I wanted to become independent and powerful and compensate with good deeds so that my own life could begin. But I failed in everything.'

He looked at Dounia and saw a face full of sorrow and pity. He had to admit that he had caused the misfortune of these two poor women. 'It's time for me to go. Please don't follow me. Go to our mother instead and stay with her. Be confident that although I'm a murderer, I'll try to live a courageous life, and I'll try to do what's right and good. But now, goodbye.'

The brother and sister left the building together and parted in the street. Having gone some distance, they both looked back and their eyes met, but Raskolnikoff gestured impatiently to make her continue and then he disappeared around the next corner.

The young man went directly to Sonia's room, to meet his fate. The girl, who had spent most of the day worrying about his safety, gave a little cry of joy when she saw him at her door, but after looking at his face she grew pale.

'Yes,' said Raskolnikoff, with a smile, 'I have come to bear the cross, Sonia. Why do you look so alarmed? It was you who advised me to make a public confession and now I'm ready. Won't the police be surprised? I just wish that my nerves would calm down — but anyway, where are the crosses?'

Sonia remained silent as she searched for her two crosses, not believing that Raskolnikoff was completely sincere about planning to confess. Nevertheless, she hung the wooden one around his neck as she made the sign of the cross with her hand.

'This was my purpose in coming here, Sonia,' Raskolnikoff began again. 'I wanted you to know that I'm going to do as you wished. I'll soon be in prison.'

By this time, Sonia was crying, but she managed to say, 'Please make the sign of the cross and say a short prayer.'

'I will, Sonia, I'll say many sincere prayers — but what are you doing?' he asked, as he saw that Sonia was preparing to go outside. 'I don't want you to come with me. Goodbye!'

Many thoughts filled Raskolnikoff's head as he descended the stairs: 'Has the game really ended? Do I have no other choice left? Why did I visit Sonia? To tell her I was going to the police or to tell her I loved her? Nonsense! I wanted her tears, and I wanted her to stop me, to give me more time. How could I ever have thought that I was some kind of hero — I, who am such a worthless coward.'

As he crossed the bridge, he thought, 'In a week or a month, I'll be crossing this bridge again in a prison van, being taken somewhere far away to begin my sentence. What will my thoughts and feelings be like on that day?'

The square, when Raskolnikoff reached it, was crowded,

but he pushed his way through and found the area with the greatest number of people. He remembered Sonia's words: 'Go immediately to the nearest public square and fall to your knees. Kiss the earth, which you have stained, and shout to everyone, "I am a murderer!" ' Sincere sorrow filled his heart, and his eyes filled with tears. With a feeling of great joy, he knelt in the very middle of the place, bowed towards the earth and kissed the muddy ground, seeking redemption.

'Look at him!' a young lad shouted. 'He must be one of those religious madmen.'

'He's very young. Do you think he's drunk?' another asked.

Realizing that he was the centre of attention, Raskolnikoff found it impossible to say, 'I am a murderer.' Instead, he stood up and began walking in the direction of the police station, but not before he caught sight of Sonia standing behind a column watching him. She was, he understood, his forever, willing to stand beside him through his greatest trials and to accompany him to the ends of the earth.

As he walked along, he reminded himself that he could still change his mind, but he continued on his way even though his legs were trembling and his heart was pounding. He made his way up the stairs and walked through the waiting area into the office of Nicodemus Thomich, the senior officer. Thomich was not in his office today, but Raskolnikoff was able to speak to Elia Petrovitch Powder, another officer that he had met once before.

'Hello! Are you visiting us?' asked Powder. 'There's no one around, but can I help you . . .? Excuse me . . . your name . . .?'

'Raskolnikoff, Rodion Romanovitch.'

'Yes, yes, of course. Don't think that I've forgotten you. I'm just not very good with names. You're a brilliant young writer, aren't you? Both my wife and I love books – she's always reading the latest work on art or literature. Anyway, what can I do for you? I heard that your mother and sister have joined you in

St Petersburg. I've even had the pleasure of meeting your sister at a little party at Razoumikhin's flat.

'I'm very sorry that your last visit to this office didn't go so well, but please accept my apology from the entire office,' Powder continued and then told Raskolnikoff about the latest gossip in the police department.

'We had an interesting case of suicide this morning. What was the name of the gentleman who blew his brains out this morning?' he shouted to his clerk in the next room

'Svidrigaïloff,' came the answer from behind the door.

Raskolnikoff went cold and in a quiet, trembling voice asked, 'Svidrigaïloff has committed suicide?'

'What! Did you know him?'

'Yes, I did. My sister worked as a governess in his family, and I met him here in St Petersburg.'

'Interesting that they found a note in his pocket which read: "I die in possession of a healthy mind; let no one, therefore, be accused of my death." They say he was a very wealthy widower. Did you have any idea that he might commit suicide?'

'I saw him yesterday. He was drinking – but I didn't suspect anything of the sort.'

'Are you all right? You seem to be getting pale again. There isn't much air in this room . . . It's so hot . . .'

'I must go,' Raskolnikoff interrupted. 'I shouldn't waste your time.'

'Nonsense! It's been a pleasure to see you,' said Powder. 'Come back for a chat any time.'

Raskolnikoff walked out of the door and down the stairs, holding on to the wall to keep himself from falling. He went outside and across the yard, and then he saw Sonia, pale as death, watching him. He stopped opposite her and smiled. Then he turned around, walked back into the police station and up the stairs to the same office on the second floor.

'Have you forgotten something?' Powder asked as Raskolnikoff entered his office. 'You look terrible! Please sit down, drink some water.'

But the young man pushed the offered glass of water to one side and in a low but distinct voice, with several interruptions, made the following statement: '*It was I who killed, with a hatchet, the old moneylender and her sister, Elizabeth, and robbery was my motive.*'

Elia Petrovitch Powder called for help and a number of police officers rushed in from different directions. Raskolnikoff repeated his confession.

Epilogue   Resurrection

A year and a half had passed since the murders, and for nine months now Raskolnikoff had been in prison in Siberia, the most isolated area of Russia.

Justice had moved quickly after Raskolnikoff's confession. Standing before the judges, he willingly told the court every detail of his crime, and finally described the exact position of the rock under which he had hidden the old woman's money and jewellery. The judges were astonished to learn that he had not even opened Alena Ivanovna's purse and had no idea how much money it contained.

The psychological experts, on the other hand, were not surprised and put forward the theory of temporary insanity as the cause of the murders. They believed that this theory, very popular at the time, removed the need to find a motive and also explained the murderer's lack of interest in what he had stolen.

When asked about his motives, though, Raskolnikoff replied that he had murdered because he wanted a new start. He thought that he would find at least 3,000 roubles in the old moneylender's flat, which would allow him to begin his career in law. But after committing the murders, he had regretted his crime. This explanation, the confession, the psychologists' theories, and his friends' accounts of his illness, depression and poverty in the months before the murders, led the judges to give Raskolnikoff a much lighter sentence than might have been expected for a double murder.

After the sentence had been pronounced, Dounia, Razoumikhin and Sonia visited him in jail. Razoumikhin was full of plans for the future for him and Dounia; they would soon be married and were considering the idea of moving to Siberia in a few years to be nearer to Raskolnikoff during his eight years of hard labour. They also reported that Pulcheria Alexandrovna's health was worrying them, and this particular information alone made the prisoner anxious.

With Sonia, Raskolnikoff remained distant and silent, but both of them knew that she would use some of the interest from Svidrigaïloff's money to enable her to accompany Raskolnikoff to Siberia when it was time for him to be moved there.

Pulcheria Alexandrovna lived long enough to see her daughter marry Dmitri Prokovitch Razoumikhin two months after Raskolnikoff had been taken to Siberia, but then she gradually became more confused and sad. She knew that something serious had happened to her son, although she was never told the truth, but she read his published article again and again, telling anyone who would listen that he would be a famous man one day. She became weaker and more depressed and finally fell ill with a fever. Within a fortnight she was dead.

Sonia kept Dounia and Razoumikhin informed about Raskolnikoff's life in prison, as well as supplying them with money on a regular basis. In her monthly letter to them she gave a complete account of the condition of their unhappy brother: his health was satisfactory, he performed his duties as instructed, and he accepted his fate without complaint. Sonia was able to speak to him on special visiting days, when he was often silent or even rude to her, and otherwise she could watch him from a distance on ordinary days when he, with a group of other prisoners, was working outside the prison walls.

Sonia had found work mending and making clothes, and soon her sewing skills became important to the whole area. She did not tell Dounia and Razoumikhin that she had spent some of her money to persuade the authorities at the prison to lighten Raskolnikoff's work load and to provide him with a healthier diet. But even with this relatively easier life, Raskolnikoff fell dangerously ill and was moved to the prison hospital.

He was kept in the hospital for a very long time, but his illness had not been caused by prison life, hard labour, rags for clothes or his shaven head. He became ill from wounded pride because, rather than feeling sorry for what he had done, he was angry with himself for having done it so badly. Like extraordinary men of the past, his conscience was clear; but unlike them, his actions had achieved nothing and therefore he had been wrong to carry them out. He wished that he could feel regret for his deeds, rather than just be bothered by their failure to prove his theory, but he could not.

He also regretted his weakness in postponing his confession. Why had he not confessed immediately or, later, committed suicide? These questions tortured him and made him wonder at his fellow prisoners' love for life. What, he asked himself, did he have to look forward to when he finished his sentence at the age of thirty-two? Would he ever again have a clear goal in life and be ready to sacrifice himself for a great idea, as he once had?

He was not liked by the other prisoners because he was silent and unfriendly. 'You're a gentleman,' they would say, disgusted despite their greater crimes. 'It wasn't a very gentlemanly act to kill two women with a hatchet.' They also attacked him because he did not believe in God. But although they saw her only rarely, they all loved Sonia and knew her history. They could see that she was kind and loving, and she often helped them in little ways, for example by writing letters, finding medicine or bringing them parcels or money from their wives and mothers.

While Raskolnikoff was in the prison hospital, Sonia was unable to visit him, but she would stand outside his hospital window each evening for a short time. Then one evening she did not appear at her usual time; Raskolnikoff became alarmed when her absence continued for days. Finally, he was released from the hospital and received a note from Sonia, explaining that she was ill and could not leave her lodgings. He felt his heart beat quickly and found it difficult to breathe.

A few days later, Raskolnikoff was strong enough to go out to work with the other prisoners, but after a few hours had to rest. He was sitting alone on a log near the river when Sonia came up and sat by his side. She was still very pale and thin from her illness, but she held out her hand and looked into his eyes. Raskolnikoff took her hand and then suddenly fell at her feet, crying and holding on to her. The girl was frightened at first, but when Raskolnikoff looked up at her she could see, and did not doubt, that he loved her – at last!

Neither of them could speak and there were tears in their eyes, but they both understood that this moment signalled the dawn of a resurrection to a new life. Love and affection surrounded them, and their hearts became as one. There still remained seven more years of pain and suffering, but so much happiness as well! Raskolnikoff was saved. He knew it. And she – she was part of his life! Life – full, real, true life was coming. They would pay for it by much patience and suffering, but it would be theirs.

Now a new story can begin, a story of the gradual rebirth of a man and his slow but certain redemption.

ACTIVITIES

Chapter 1

Before you read

1 Name two Russian novels or plays and their authors. What do you know about them? What do you expect a nineteenth-century Russian novel to be like?

2 The main character in this novel, Rodion Romanovitch Raskolnikoff, believes that there are two groups of men in society: ordinary men and extraordinary men. Write a list of adjectives that might describe each group.

3 Check the definitions of the words in *italics* below in the Word List at the back of this book, and then answer these questions.

  a What is a typical rate of *interest* on a bank loan in your country?

  b Explain the relationship of a *step*brother to a *step*sister.

  c Are pictures of a *skull* used to represent something pleasant or unpleasant? Give an example of the use of this symbol.

  d Can you name any children's stories or films which have *witches* or *governesses* in them? Are these characters usually good or bad? In what way?

  e What kinds of experience make your heart *pound*? List some examples.

  f List the types of buildings where you would expect to find a *porter* in your country. What are a porter's responsibilities?

4 Explain how these words can be connected with poverty:
   drunkard   filthy   louse   pawn   prostitute   sacrifice

While you read

5 The events in Chapter 1 take place over three days. On which day does Raskolnikoff perform each of these actions? Write 1st, 2nd or 3rd.

  a He sews a piece of cloth inside his coat.   . . . . .

  b He leaves money for Marmeladoff's family.   . . . . .

  c He reads a letter from his mother.   . . . . .

101

   d He pawns his father's watch.   . . . . .

   e He takes a hatchet from the porter's hut.   . . . . .

   f He hears Elizabeth's plans for the next evening.   . . . . .

6 Write the name of the person who is being described.

   a old and thin with a suspicious look   . . . .

   b a poor, generous, optimistic student   . . . .

   c no beard or moustache, thin grey hair,
       yellow skin   . . . .

   d tall, shy, awkward and not very clever   . . . .

   e young, proud, serious and handsome
       with dark hair and eyes   . . . .

After you read

7 What is the relationship between these pairs of people? Explain why you think the relationship is good or bad.

   a Raskolnikoff and Pulcheria Alexandrovna

   b Raskolnikoff and Razoumikhin

   c Marmeladoff and Catherine Ivanovna

   d Alena Ivanovna and Elizabeth

8 Work with a partner. Discuss three things that happen by chance to Raskolnikoff which he believes control his fate. How do these three events lead to murder?

Chapter 2

Before you read

9 Describe how you think Raskolnikoff will act and feel on the day after he commits two murders.

While you read

10 Where is Raskolnikoff each of the four times he decides to confess to the murders?

   a . . . .

   b . . . .

   c . . . .

   d . . . .

11 Put these places in the order (1–7) that Raskolnikoff visits them in Chapter 2.

a	Marmeladoff and Catherine Ivanovna's room	. . . . .
b	a café for tea and newspapers	. . . . .
c	the police station	. . . . .
d	Razoumikhin's flat during a party	. . . . .
e	a ruined building in a courtyard	. . . . .
f	Alena Ivanovna's flat	. . . . .
g	Razoumikhin's flat for a chat	. . . . .

After you read

12 Make two lists: in the first, give reasons why Raskolnikoff should be able to avoid being accused of the murders; in the second, give reasons why people might begin to suspect Raskolnikoff of the murders.

13 In what circumstances is blood referred to in Chapter 2? Why is it an important symbol in this story?

Chapter 3

Before you read

14 Work with a partner. Discuss what you know about Alena Ivanovna and Marmeladoff. In your opinion, whose life is more valuable? If only one of the two could live, who should it be?

15 Which of these characters do you think should have a guilty conscience and which should have a clear conscience? Why?

Raskolnikoff   Dounia   Marmeladoff   Sonia   Razoumikhin

While you read

16 Describe how Raskolnikoff feels in each of these situations. Write two adjectives.

a	Seeing his mother and sister in his room after a separation of three years.	. . . .
b	Next morning when his mother and sister visit him in his room.	. . . .
c	Walking from his lodgings to Porphyrius Petrovitch's office.	. . . .

d In Porphyrius Petrovitch's office. . . . .

e Outside his building with his accuser. . . . .

17 According to Raskolnikoff's theory, mark each of these features either O for ordinary men or E for extraordinary men.

a They follow the laws of the land. . . . . .

b They have a right to break laws and destroy the existing order if their acts benefit mankind. . . . . .

c They are guided by their conscience. . . . . .

d They are inferior and obedient. . . . . .

e They are born to produce children and maintain normal life. . . . . .

f They are independent thinkers who break down barriers and change the world. . . . . .

After you read

18 How are these people described in this chapter?

a Pulcheria

b Dounia

c Sonia

d Svidrigaïloff

e Porphyrius Petrovitch

19 Discuss why Raskolnikoff feels frightened and worried at the end of Chapter 3.

Chapter 4

Before you read

20 In your opinion, is Porphyrius Petrovitch certain that Raskolnikoff is the murderer? Why (not)?

While you read

21 Mark each statement T (true) or F (false).

a Dounia and Svidrigaïloff will both benefit financially from Marfa's death. . . . . .

b Svidrigaïloff approves of Looshin as a husband
for Dounia.   . . . . .

c Looshin believes he has been insulted by both
Raskolnikoff and his mother.   . . . . .

d Dounia appears to be very unhappy when her
engagement to Looshin is broken.   . . . . .

e Razoumikhin accompanies Raskolnikoff to Sonia's
lodgings.   . . . . .

f Sonia's faith in God is very strong.   . . . . .

g Porphyrius Petrovitch's friendly chat upsets Raskolnikoff. . . . . .

h The painter, Nikola, is Porphyrius Petrovitch's
planned surprise.   . . . . .

i Raskolnikoff is cheered up by Nikola's confession
and Porphyrius Petrovitch's impatience.   . . . . .

j Raskolnikoff's mysterious accuser saw him on the
night Alena was murdered.   . . . . .

After you read

22 Match the people with something they *might* have thought.
Svidrigaïloff   Raskolnikoff   Razoumikhin   Looshin   Sonia
Porphyrius   Petrovitch

a 'What a relief to get away from all the love and understanding from my mother and sister!'

b 'I will protect Dounia from every danger, especially from the man who almost ruined her reputation. I love her!'

c 'I expect I'll find out something about the murder case from this visit, but I'll go slowly and not frighten him.'

d 'Perhaps I encouraged Marfa to eat and drink too much on the night she died, but that's not murder.'

e 'Sonia offers me my only hope of redemption.'

f 'I cannot believe that a poor girl like Dounia would break our engagement.'

g 'I must see Dounia. Surely she'll be tempted by my 10,000 roubles.'

h 'I must make him understand that God can help him too.'

Chapter 5

Before you read

23 Work with a partner. Can you think of any motives for murder that you would approve of, or at least excuse?

While you read

24 Circle the correct answer.

   a Raskolnikoff is Catherine's *most/least* favourite guest.

   b Catherine's plans for the future are *practical/unreal.*

   c Sonia reacts *cruelly/sympathetically* to the news that Raskolnikoff is Elizabeth's killer.

   d Raskolnikoff's greatest hope is that Sonia *will/won't* leave him.

   e Raskolnikoff committed murder mainly because he wanted to be *rich/extraordinary.*

   f Sonia advises Raskolnikoff to *confess/leave St Petersburg.*

   g Raskolnikoff thinks he will *never/soon* be arrested.

   h Dounia *believes/doesn't believe* that Raskolnikoff is guilty of murder.

   i The blood on Catherine Ivanovna's clothes is from *a cut/her lungs.*

   j *Svidrigaïloff/Raskolnikoff* will pay for Catherine Ivanovna's funeral.

After you read

25 Work with a partner. Act out an appropriate conversation between one of these pairs of people.

   a Catherine Ivanovna and Raskolnikoff, sitting next to each other at the meal after Marmeladoff's funeral.

   b Dounia and Razoumikhin, after Dounia visits Raskolnikoff in his room.

   c Two strangers, watching Catherine Ivanovna and her children in the street near the bridge.

   d Two of Sonia's neighbours after they witness Catherine Ivanovna's death.

Chapter 6

Before you read

26 Work with a partner. The title of this chapter is 'Fate'. Discuss what you think Raskolnikoff's fate will be.

While you read

27 Who is it? Write the name of the character who:

a   sleeps outside under a tree one night.   ………………..

b   worries when she finds Raskolnikoff's room
      empty.   ………………..

c   has received a mysterious letter.   ………………..

d   has confessed to the murders to the police.   ………………..

e   accuses Raskolnikoff of being the murderer
      based on the evidence he has collected.   ………………..

f   is carrying a gun when she meets
      Svidrigaïloff.   ………………..

g   provides for Catherine Ivanovna's children
      and for Sonia.   ………………..

h   sees Svidrigaïloff shoot himself.   ………………..

i   places a cross round Raskolnikoff's neck.   ………………..

j   leaves a suicide note.   ………………..

After you read

28 How do these people show their love for Raskolnikoff?
Pulcheria   Razoumikhin   Dounia   Sonia

29 Who gives Raskolnikoff this advice?

a   'Consider escaping to America as soon as possible.'

b   'I recommend that you go to the police and confess to the murders.'

c   'Your confession will wash away half your crime.'

d   'Make the sign of the cross and say a short prayer.'

e   'Sit down. Drink some water.'

Epilogue

Before you read

30 Work with a partner. How many different types of motive can you think of for committing murder? Do you think Raskolnikoff's motive is typical of most murderers or not?

While you read

31 List five possible reasons why Raskolnikoff got a relatively light sentence for his crime.

    a ....

    b ....

    c ....

    d ....

    e ....

After you read

32 Discuss these questions.

    a Does Raskolnikoff get the punishment he deserves?

    b Explain why it is not necessary to find a motive for a crime if the criminal uses the defence of temporary insanity.

    c What regrets does Raskolnikoff have?

    d What happens to Sonia, Razoumikhin, Dounia and her mother after Raskolnikoff goes to prison?

    e Why is this section of the book called 'Resurrection'?

    f Who or what is responsible for Raskolnikoff's return to life?

Writing

33 Write a newspaper article based on either Raskolnikoff's arrest or Raskolnikoff's trial and sentencing. Include an appropriate newspaper-style heading.

34 Write an article for a legal journal (read by lawyers and other professionals) explaining why Porphyrius Petrovitch is a great investigating magistrate.

35 Imagine that you are Raskolnikoff. Write about events and your feelings on three important days in your life in your private diary.

36 Imagine that you are Pulcheria Alexandrovna. It is shortly after Raskolnikoff has been sent to Siberia. Write a conversation between you and a new neighbour in St Petersburg. Tell your neighbour about your children, whom you love and are proud of.

37 Imagine that you are a psychologist who has Raskolnikoff as a patient during his trial. Write a report on him, explaining why you think he is not mad, and give reasons why you think he has a split personality.

38 Write a conversation that one of these pairs of people might have had on the occasion indicated.

    a Pulcheria and Dounia, after Pulcheria sees Raskolnikoff for the last time.

    b Sonia and a priest, after Raskolnikoff tells her that he murdered Alena Ivanovna and her stepsister, Elizabeth.

    c Svidrigaïloff and the soldier, just before the widower commits suicide.

    d Raskolnikoff and Sonia, after he accepts her love and they can look forward to a new life together.

39 Imagine that you are Sonia. It is two years since Raskolnikoff finished his prison sentence. Write a letter telling Dounia and Razoumikhin about your new life together.

40 You teach English literature to schoolchildren. Write a lecture explaining the purpose of the Epilogue in this novel to your students.

41 You want to persuade a group of investors to put money into your project to make *Crime and Punishment* into a film. Make a list of reasons why it would make a good film. Suggest which actors you would want to play the leading roles.

42 Write a letter to a good friend who has asked you to recommend a book to take on holiday. Tell your friend why he or she should or should not take *Crime and Punishment*.

WORD LIST

blush (v) to become red in the face, usually because you are embarrassed

bolt (n/v) a metal bar that slides across to lock a door or window

conscience (n) the feelings that tell you whether your behaviour is morally right or wrong

drunkard (n) someone who often gets drunk

epilogue (n) a piece of writing added to the end of a book

fate (n) a power that is believed to control what happens in people's lives

filthy (adj) extremely dirty

governess (n) a woman who lived with a family and taught the children at home, especially in the past

hatchet (n) a short-handled tool with a metal blade for cutting wood

interest (n) money charged by a bank or moneylender when you borrow money

interpret (v) to explain the meaning of an event, statement or idea

lining (n) a piece of material covering the inside of something such as a jacket, coat or box

lodgings (n) a room or rooms in someone's house that you pay rent to live in

louse (n) a very small insect that lives on the skin and hair of animals and people

magistrate (n) a civil officer with responsibility for the investigation of crimes and administration of the law

pawn (v) to leave a valuable object with a moneylender so that you can borrow money from them

porter (n) someone whose job is to take care of a building

pound (v) to beat quickly and loudly

prostitute (n) someone who has sex to earn money

redemption (n) the state of being saved from the power of evil, especially according to the Christian religion

resurrection (n) rebirth after death; the resurrection of Jesus Christ is one of the main beliefs of the Christian religion

sacrifice (n/v) the act of giving up something important or valuable in order to get something that is more important

sentence (n) a punishment that a judge gives to someone who is guilty of a crime

skull (n) the bones of a person's or an animal's head